Out from the Shadows

OUT FROM THE SHADOWS
Poetic Portraits of Faith

Copyright © 2007 J. R. O'Neill. All rights reserved. Except for brief quotations in critical articles or reviews, no part of this book may be reproduced in any manner without prior written permission from the publisher. Write: Permissions, Wipf and Stock Publishers, 199 W. 8th Ave., Suite 3, Eugene, OR 97401.

Wipf & Stock Publishers
199 West 8th Avenue, Suite 3
Eugene, Oregon 97401

ISBN 13: 978-1-55635-177-8

Manufactured in the U.S.A.

"*Out from the Shadows: Poetic Portraits of Faith* brings a clear message: GOD HAS FAITH IN US! These poems speak to my inner being. They help me connect with my own life's journey. Validity, Discovery, Community, Futurity take the reader on a voyage from the depths of despair, to healing ahas!, sharing moments with others, to pointing the glorious way to God!"

—Mary R. Knutson
Educator and Friend
Minneapolis MN

"Depression and addiction—two great battles of our times. With courage and candor, O'Neill faces these battles head on offering hope to all those who journey through the dark night of the soul. Dawn comes through the grace and power of God's presence, the embrace of family and friends and looking for the miraculous in simple, every day moments of life. I love some of the one-liners in the book. My favorite: 'Let's party at your house demon free.'"

—Betsy Lee, President
Prayer Ventures
Bloomington, MN

"J. R. O'Neill has written a book of comfort and compassion for those who struggle with what fate and choice have made of their lives. His pieces speak from a personal voice, and a collective one, celebrating what true and humble faith can give to souls in torment."

—Deborah Keenan
Professor, Faculty Advisor and Poet
Masters of Fine Arts Program
Hamline University, St. Paul, MN

"The powerful imagery in O'Neill's *Out of the Shadows Poetic Portraits of Faith* creates a stark but hopeful description of the challenges and discoveries along the journey from addiction to recovery and beyond."

—Ruth and Stephen Klein
Teacher and Director of
Community Emergency Assistance Program
Brooklyn Park, MN

Out from the Shadows
Poetic Portraits of Faith

J. R. O'Neill

Illustrations by
Jerry Amon

Resource *Publications*
An imprint of *Wipf and Stock Publishers*
199 West 8th Avenue • Eugene OR 97401

*To fellow sojourners
in and coming
out from the shadows
of depression
and
addiction*

---

*Special thanks
to my loving and ever supportive wife, Denise,
my colorful, artistic friend, Jerry Amon,
members of Cross of Glory Lutheran Church's Poetry Circle
and in memory of Doug Clark*

Table of Contents

Preface ix

Validity 1
    Reflection/Discussion Questions 62

Discovery 63
    Reflection/Discussion Questions 96

Community 97
    Reflection/Discussion Questions 127

Futurity 129
    Reflection/Discussion Questions 151

Notes on Poems 153
Index of Titles 171

Preface

Poetry and art in general always seemed to be the prize possession of the upper class and privileged. Growing up the son of a factory worker, our family troubled by my father's alcoholism and mental illness, I could only joke about being a poet and wish I might draw a bit better.

Still the power of words was clear to me even as a child. Today I have come to realize that words are the means of both receiving and giving what is profoundly personal, wonderful and mysterious. Words help create, affirm, validate and deepen relationships. Words provide a livelihood empowering even the lowliest to become a valuable artist and an instrument of God's grace.

While I have discovered painting word pictures is a gift about which I have become passionate, any talent I may have for drawing remains unquestionably hidden. That's why I am so grateful for the artistic ability and heart my friend Jerry Amon brings to this project. Together we have combined preferred means of image making into a recipe we hope will feed the soul.

Intended for broad readership, we are especially mindful of those struggling to find hope and joy in their lives. It is our desire that this book will invite you on your own journey out from the shadows. While many have expressed appreciation for the "Notes on Poems" included in the back of this book, we are aware that by including these comments we run the risk of severely limiting the worth of each poem. For this reason we encourage you to let the poetry and drawings speak for themselves allowing you to read your own lives into the artful mix. To that end we humbly offer to you what God has first given us and we pray that you may more fully enjoy the heights and depths of soulful living.

Validity

In the darkest moments of the soul, one encounters a compelling force that calls for crucial and complete transparency. When that force is found to be warm and life-giving, the capacity to own one's own shadow is born.

Pilot Me

Oh, that longest of journeys
        Into the depths of my being
That discovery voyage
        Through vast shadows beyond seeing

Yes, I have a need to go
        Yet, still I am afraid to know
But if I stay where I am
        Then I will most certainly die

Pilot me, Lord, to enter
        This strange, wonderful world within
Toward that culmination
        Of my life lived free from sin.

Shame in the Weather

Dark clouds form on the horizon
Dull ache and deep rumbling fear
Welling up inside me again
Shooting bolts that cause me to jerk
As though I am in clear danger
Of being struck dead on the ground
That worst of storms about to hit
My shame exposed, seen as valid

From above comes a clear, calm voice
Your fears don't cause the weather front
My son stirs up the flash and rain
The wind gives you air to breath
And blows new life to meet your need
I am with you, for you—always!
Let those clouds draw you close to me
Your shame I'll change to balmy days

Shifting Shadow

Love welcomed me
Yet I drew back
Torn by what I see
Scorned by what I lack

Shadow shifting
Within and without
Drawn by what I know
Conned by what I doubt

Evil attacks
The weakest link
Shadow revolts
Storm makes me sink

Once, twice, three times
I'm out!
Out in the dark, yet
I see light!

Oh, brother Judas
Oh, brother Mark
There *is* a way
Out from the dark!

Oh, sister Mary
Oh, sister Jane
Risk coming back
In spite of the pain

Flame burning brightly
The darkest of night
I seen worth saving
Cry wrong or what's right?

Two shifting figures
Light shines in the dark
One moves to wholeness
One the devil's dart

Legion at the Crossroads

Legion at the crossroads
On a hunt among votive stones
Union of opposites
Split image of heaven and hell
Site of divination
Seeking life beyond what one knows
Ghost that haunts or Spirit that heals
How can this poor soul tell?

Should have! Would have! Could have!
Inner voice screams condemnation
Dare not! Can not! Will not!
That knee-jerk negativity!
How I'm longing for life!
Imprisoned, fragmented, I'm done!
Those nasty chains of doubt and fear
Nothing is able to free me!

Guilt and shame rule my life
Approval won't ease my burdens
Feelings scream: "Terrible!"
And I believe I'm terrible
Shadow shouts: "You're insane!"
Insane? Hey, I'm just plain hurting!
All right, I know I'm powerless
Those monsters! They're lethal!

Lips quivering, tears flow
Smell of body bleeding with sweat
Dark soul in broad daylight
Must life be filled with such madness?
Sunlight speaks: "You have voice!
Don't give in to those demons yet
One word from me and life is blessed
I'll be your sure defense."

Be gone, evil spirits!
Like mad cows plunge into the sea!
Heart of child, take courage
From fear comes opportunity
Anxiety undone!
Satan's choice-killers are stunned
Dance, you seekers among the tombs!
March to the beat of a different drum!

Winter's Thaw

Jack Frost gone evil
    Jammed feelings numb
Throne of God chilled
    Joy frozen

Flash of sharp glass
    Fling to the rocks
Jagged edge catches
    Flesh cut

Blood flows freely
    Bolting in fear
First-aid to finger
    Bleeding stopped

Heart is still warm
    High the concern
Bright sun shining
    Hope returns

Healing begins
    Home is restored
Highway to health
    Heartfelt soul

Grief comes swiftly
    Good in old ways
Helped us cope once
    Got us stuck

Off with the old
    On with the new
Gift is prepared
    Old won't do

Loss of what's known
    Lingers and hurts
Oh, but One knows
    Love prevails

Bled on a tree
    Bad meant for good
Life isn't lived
    Before blood

Feelings will flow
    Fresh from the Heart
Back away thoughts
    Fight quick flight

No pain no gain
    Not afraid now
Found in the fear
    Nerve of steel

Layers of skin
    Levels of function
Never simple
    Light knows all

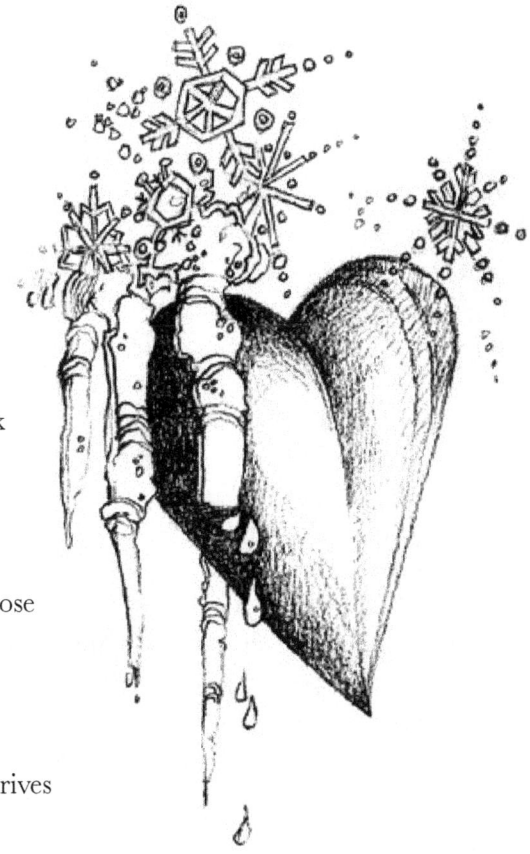

Shadows serve us
    Stir in the dark
Living by faith
    Shalom rings

Re-relate, Self
    Rhythm cut loose
Separate yet
    Really one

Letting go now
    Loosed soul thrives
Ripped by tension
    Life expands

Blood brother come
    Blood sister too
Libation heals
    Bold blood gives . . .

Greatest value
    Gotten from God
Bought with crowned cross
    Gone thick skin

Flesh gives way to
    Fuller acceptance
Gem at the core
    Floodlight shines

Wise to wait now
    Want given to will
Fear fades with the
    Winter's Thaw

Monstrous Love

Suddenly awakened, eyes wide open, heart racing
    Who is it? What woke me up? Why am I so scared?
Mom! Dad! I'm not a fool. It's a ghoul all right
    Just outside my room at the end of the hallway!
I can see it starring at me through the doorway
    I'm afraid it's going to bite me
Won't you come and chase it away—
        Please!

Silence—just the sound of the blood rushing through my veins
    And the sight of those beady eyes starring at me
Mom! Dad! Come help me. I can't sleep.
    I know it's just a little mark on the woodwork but
It has power over me at night and it won't go away
    Can't you come and cover it? Or just maybe
You could keep me safe in your bed tonight—
        Please!

I can't stand this anymore! I've got to kill that monster!
    Where is my popgun? I lost the cork but I can hit it hard!
Take that you nasty beast! You fiend that feasts
    On fair little girls and boys like me. Be gone you brute!
There! I've smashed it good! I don't see it starring at me anymore
    With those hungry eyes and that pointy, quiet tongue
Is it gone? I think so. I hope so…
        Please!

Awakened again, eyes wide open, heart racing
        Who is it? What woke me up? Why am I so scared?
Honey, I'm no fool. It's a ghoul all right
        Feels like it's going to eat me up alive!
How strange for this middle-age man to be so deathly afraid
        And it's not just happening when I try to sleep
Tell me why this demon is tormenting me day and night!
                Please!

I didn't kill it did I? That monster from my childhood
        It just slipped from the woodwork into my soul
And now I am utterly bound by its lies and deception
        Helpless in overcoming its debilitating grip on my life!
What a goon to think I could handle it all on my own!
        As though I had the power to destroy this freakish force
Go ahead, you ugly ogre! Go ahead and say it, "Shame on you!" If you
                Please!

No! I won't play fool to this ghoul and forget the lamp in the hallway
        Away dark, frantic, cowardly reactions! Though frightened again
The Light flames bright into the depths of my being
        An omnipresent, all-powerful, perfect cosmic parent
One who neither slumbers nor sleeps; who will keep my life
        Whose truth will heal and save me from shame
O Monstrous Love, every child's dragon slayer, let me rest in your peace
                Please!

Black Hole

Round the rim of a deep, black hole
      I walk the line that saves my soul
Void whips me and the way slips me
      Oh, how I fear I'll fall for sure!
Shepherd steady, ever ready
      Come now and make my steps secure!
Out shout the voice that sinks my heart
      Inspire the choice that beats the dark!

Gospel Light

Two ends of one battery
    Bi-pole source of energy
        Goal—Power to move
            light over darkness
        Two ends of eternity
    Tri-pole force of Trinity
Goal—Power to choose

Mutinous Emotion

Mutinous emotion shakes the holy temple
      Ebullience has gone mad stirring up the simple
The spirit seeks to calm the wild, raging bother
      While the mind, mood and body rock, roll and totter

Microcosm of broken world about to sink
      Rebellion must be countered by the Master link
Epitome of a larger problem that prevails
      Eye on love's cruciform in face of betrayal

Truth revealed by a bright star and a holy crèche
Hope tames the susceptibilities of the flesh
Light shines from behind the worshipful Master's chair
Savage nerves are soothed after every devil's dare

"Be still and know that I'm in charge!" cries the captain
      Quiet voice from the deep by which one is certain
Our godhead's built upon the rock and waves alike
      All danger to one's soul now hung on cross and spike!

Biffy by the Handle

Biffy by the handle
Outhouse by the lake
Relief is in sight
Reality hard to take

Awake! Child, within me
Rise, let's take a walk
No more hiding now
It's no use to balk

Speak and I will listen
Tell your tales of woe
Share all your secrets
Learn to let them go

Biffy by the handle
Our house by the lake
Making love on hold
This is hard to take!

. . .

. . .
Medicine, counselor
Groups to make me well
Grace throughout it all
Wellness hard to tell

Guess at what is normal
Finish what's begun
Time to stop the lie
Truth can lead to fun

Biffy by the handle
Outhouse by the lake
Need for approval
Gone in the wake

Intimate with myself
Closer to my mate
Let go of control
Let God compensate

Ah, what relief this is!
No living the lie
No numbing out now
My child is wide-eyed!

Biffy by the handle
Lighthouse by the sea
Adult growing stronger
Healthy child in me

Different from others?
All of us must go
From cleaning the mess
To making us whole

Freedom to go now
Walk around the lake
Child, you are able
It's not too late!

Habits

They are the ligament of daily life
        Good and yet a source of strife
Most dispositions are quick to be learned
        But hard fast and slow to turn

So if a godly life is your desire
        Be wise 'bout those you acquire
And pray patience for the time it will take
        To let go of those you hate

Take Heart

Take heart, get up!
He is calling you
Eyes may not see
But heart hears His voice
Mind can't believe
But soul knows who heals

Bruised reed—bowed, bent
Something has happened
Harsh words spoken
Life knocked out of sorts
Self-doubt pokin'
Feeling like failure

Jump up, run fast!
Don't miss His coming
Feel free to ask
The Healer is listenin'
Take off the mask
Give Him room to work

Open up! Look!
Believe sight unseen
Tender His touch
To welt and weary
Loves us so much
Enjoy life at last!

Mercy Seat

Lying in bed
Mind full of dread
Fear must be shed

Up in my chair
Tell God my cares
Satan beware!

Now on my feet
Daybreak to meet
Thanks, Mercy Seat!

Pan for Gold

Troubled waters, flash of lightning
Threats thunder and life seems frightening
My inner soul shakes at its core
Yet a voice breathes calm in the storm
Filling my life with confidence
Fear takes flight. Yes, it's God again!
My Strength from within and without
Stirring faith and casting out doubt
Through all the throws of my distress
God moves to mold my godliness
Hence, across choppy waves I'll go
And at their worst
I'll pan for gold

Less Being More

Belly heavy on my belt
    Makes my aging ready felt
Active lifestyle years on end
    Still this freight from gut to chin

Oh, the constant gravity!
    I am starved to be set free!
Give me sweets and strong coffee
    Just a little energy

Yes, move this weight one more day
    Pray tell I will find a way
To lighten my load at last
    Less being more than the past

Mother Divine

I think I hear the sound of my mother
        Her heartbeat, deep breathing, flow of fluid
Warm vibrations from one like no other
        Cadence of creation stirs in womb hid

From a distance, sounds of another world
        Abrupt dissonance from poised existence
Still a safe rhythm calms her precious pearl
        This home within her like a sure defense

With each beat of her heart I hear God say
        "Welcome my dear. Please know that I love you.
I'll always be your safe and lighted way.
        Take heart, my child. I'm sure to see you through."

What relief for one so vulnerable!
        That a mother echoes God's perfect love
While needy herself God is still able
        To fill this frail child with life from above

Oh, blessed assurance loved sight unseen!
        Knit together by Your careful design
Whatever's to come or might well have been
        I give my all, Sweet Lord, Mother Divine!

Mother's Apron Strings

How does one cut the strings
    And not ruin the apron?
Leave mom but still not loose
    One's mothering life source?

What goes when the apron
    Has holes and splits at the seam?
How do no strings improve
    Poor cloth's sewability?

Might we try to untie
    In a give-and-take fashion
Seeking God's help to weave
    Our own rich tapestry?

God knows our limitations
    The stint of our mothers' too
Cut all but love's divine wrap
    And watch the new you show through!

Birthday Party

Did I ask or did he just offer?
Either case it came to be
That on my seventh birthday
Dad held a party for me!

We all played clothespins in the bottle
Chased musical chairs on key
Held sack races in the yard
Pin the tail on the donkey

There was much laughter and loads of fun
Yes, yummy cake and ice cream
Bright balloons for my friends but
Lord, why did I make a scene?

Perhaps just young and in need of a nap
Or just eager to impress
But I didn't win the games
And did not come out the best

Still my father showed love and patience
Though surely I deserved less
All my friends went home happy
And I was the one most blessed

Years have passed since that birthday party
Dad has long passed away too
And while memories are mixed
One thing's most certainly true

Dad loved me. He honored my birth.
This fact feels like I'm reborn!
Moving me to new freedom
Embraced and fully adorned!

Wave of Contractions

Wave of contractions, fast goes birth movement
     Into this world from the one he had known
Painful adjustments—sight, sound, excitement
     Cut from the womb, dreadful storm to be born!

Is it a girl? No, a boy. Alive? Yes.
     Has he no chin? No grin? Just bring him in!
Where is his dad? So sad! Take a blood test.
     His mom's negative but both are livin'

Blizzard blown landscape this dark winter morn
     Mother accepts giving birth on her own
Father arrives to greet son who's now born
     But finds himself lost and cold to the bone

Hear the baby crying; His mother too.
     See the tears rolling from his father's eyes
Is there joy or just deep grief running through?
     Seems with fresh birth something old now must die

All did their best still they suffered great loss
     And needed to grieve in order to heal
Nothing was perfect and so goes the Cross
Our sin's refusal to accept, to feel

'Twas that way the first day but to the end?
     Must they now suffer this unresolved grief?
Spend life in fear of being abandoned?
     Let shame take what's near and dear like a thief?

Oh, say "No!" to these infractions! And ask
     God to help and guide thee
There's new life after those old contractions
     And the best is yet to be seen!

In Your Real Presence

Ok, I have done it again
Yes, I have doubted in the dark
What you have shown me in the light
But it's hard not to trust feelings
I know you are good and loving
You are all-powerful and wise
You know the details in my life
I know that you are in control
You surely have a plan for me
That you will not abandon me
Yes, I believe you'll save my soul
But it's tough when you hide your face
So help me, Lord, rely on you
And not just on my emotions
You're right. I really need to grow
Wean me of my need for feelings
Take me to a deeper level
Let me dwell in your real presence

Cross Examination

What a beautiful cross to wear
What a challenging cross to bear!
One to see with human eyes
The other faith to recognize

Purposeful Love show me my cross
For life in Christ I'll suffer loss
Thank you, Jesus, for bearing yours
My certain way past many doors

Listen to Him!

Ouch, Malchus!
Oh, that must have hurt
When Pete's swift sword
Lopped off your ear!

Not by might
No, says the Lord! I'll
Heal a hearing
That stills your fear.

Dark Side of Moon

Born in the image but not as the sun
    When way grows dark there's no kindling the noon
Attempts breed addiction, life comes undone
    Apart from God's spark I'm dark side of moon
So, I turn once again toward my light
    And shine like the Son whether day or night

Name Change

What name does God want to give me?
Warm and Friendly seem good enough
Yet my encounters with Divine
Suggest a change is in the Wind
The Kingdom of God is at hand
I am called to fully invest
There is need for my very best
And what might God name me if I'm
Willing to engage?
Invite, Equip and Encourage
That's the change God's calling in me
That's the one I am meant to be
Help me, Oh Name above all names
To live my life as You desire

Dawn of My Real Mother

Arrows flew one bright morning amidst children at play
    No sign of Mother anywhere until
One hit me near the eye and she came without delay
    Bloody hole poked in my nose left her chilled
Her thin, tired body naked for my eyes to see
    How little and weak she appeared that day
Trying to calm and help me I just fought to let be
    So 'twas off to the doctor straightaway

There I was examined, my wound cleaned and skin sewed up
    Lost in a sea of strange hands and weird smells
While Mother stood her distance not wanting to disrupt
    She seemed to me withdrawn into a shell
And then just when we were to leave the doctor's office
    Mom, who'd been bigger than life, just fainted!
My sure foundation now like a slippery crevice
    This rock of my salvation un-sainted

Many years have passed since the dawn of my real mother
    But only now have I begun to see
The woman who birthed and raised me is like no other
    Her love, while not perfect, was right for me
True for us all the need for a real moth'ring life source
    We stumble and fall when we make mom God
Arrows will fly wildly and they strike with deadly force
    Our sure protection is the Shepherd's rod.

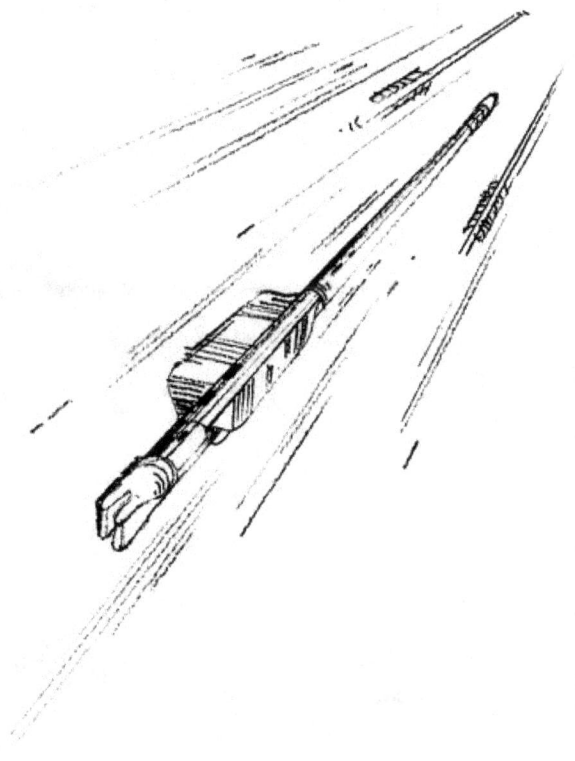

Built on The Rock

I watched in horror as my house slid into the sea
What seemed a sure foundation simply proved not to be
My life built on concavity—a weak, slipp'ry slope
When disapproval fell like hard rain I had no hope

Yet, arising out of the waters came a new me
A house built on firm ground like it was suppose to be
Accepted, secure, significant self—Yes, baptized!
The need no longer to be prized in the world's blind eyes

Built on the rock a heart can withstand condemnation
Bright soul's well-being anchored in the love of the Son
The structure wherein a life resides is light and free
When our hope is fixed on God's grace and eternity

Saved from Grandiosity

Such a simple thing to
Just hide Dad's cashed paycheck
That he might not buy drink
And they'd have food on deck

Yes, Mom, he did hide it
The best a young boy could
Believing that good deed
On him his family stood

Like a crafty serpent
Dad found the money stash
And now he's all drunked up
Turning their dreams to ash

Money's long forgotten
The family stayed in tact
But sheer grandiosity
Has set the poor child back

Who told this little boy
He had the power to save
But failed his simple task
So it's shame to the grave?

Take heart, my precious son
You weren't responsible
I was the One in charge
You were to be playful

I let him find the coin
To show your golden band
None can snatch a child from
The Father's loving hand!

Rabbouni!

Teacher, teacher, you call me by name!
    Back with what I lack on a fast track
Eyes, surprised, couldn't see, yet you came
    Warming my heart, new start—it's a fact!

Savior, Savior, you knew I would cry!
    Death, that final breath, to Thee I clutch
My pain, the same as saints from on high
    Real tears, no fears with your loving touch

Lord, Lord, still this tomb-like emptiness!
    I burn to learn what "Christ is risen!" means
Assure your might won't slight our sweet caress
    Then I'll not cling but sing these holy scenes

Save Me!

Innocence lost?
No, but my child of God is rudely tossed
Within and without, shamefully exposed
To the powers and principalities
Of that world of darkness Satan chose
Estranged from my sane, true identity

What! You're surprised?
Oh, precious love. Someone's covered your eyes!
But the problem's not a firm self to find
It's embracing one you already have
Gaining freedom from the motives that bind
By the might of God's fight on your behalf

Yes, help me trust
While forces work to reduce me to dust
And my mind grasps for false substitutes
God protect and draw me close to your heart
Secured in Christ like a deep, solid root
Save me, all you've made me, right from the start!

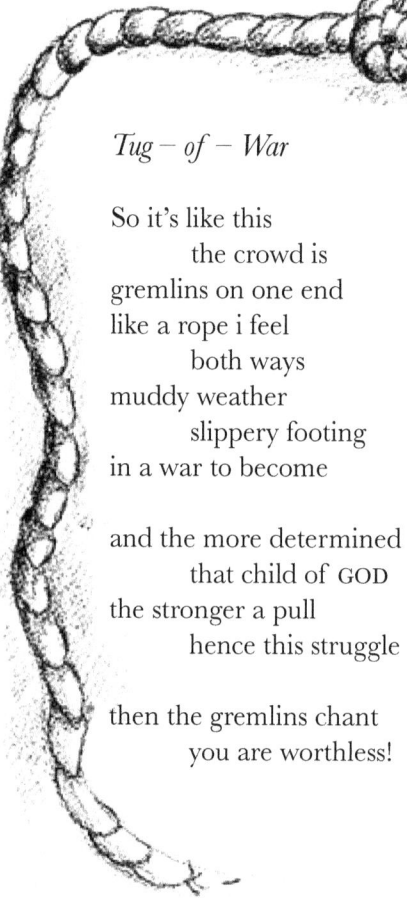

Tug – of – War

So it's like this
    the crowd is
gremlins on one end
like a rope i feel
    both ways
muddy weather
    slippery footing
in a war to become

and the more determined
    that child of GOD
the stronger a pull
    hence this struggle

then the gremlins chant
    you are worthless!

we are the champions

today
    hushed
angels on the other
p u l l e d
    at once
of the mind
    messy
a whole person

i am to be
    i'm told i am
by my enemy
    of the inner man

as the angels hang on
you're a fake!
you have nothing to offer
you are weak,
undesirable, unlovable
a joke!
and you're going to loose

oh, but what's that music   in your other ear?
    a litany of
    angelic voices
    crying
    GOD is near!
those gremlins seem   formidable but
    THE ALMIGHTY   is on your side
calling you now   unto firm, holy ground!

i know this to be true
the farther those gremlins   try to yank me their way
    the deeper GOD   draws me home to stay!
so I focus on what's real—   that lasting, unambiguous,
    love
    of
    JESUS!

and just when it seems   this war never ends
CHRIST joins hands and leans   a strong tug that wins!

Found

Swept unto the rocks
      Unexpectedly
My innermost parts
      Weak and floundering

Lost, my soul to die
      So remarkably
Sure help hears my cry
      And God does find me!

Curl Unfurled

I was spinning
    Spinning out of control
Caught in winning
    Winning every lost soul
Work was piling
    Piling well past my reach
I just filing
    Filing dead words to preach

All was sailing
    Sailing off into orbit
My hands flailing
    Flailing heart in dark pit
Then came closing
    Closing round my crazed world
A voice posing
    Posing: Let curl unfurl

No more clutching
    Clutching saintly desires
Turn to touching
    Touching soul's wind and fire
For there's nothing
    Nothing past God's control
In those loving
    Loving arms grace will hold

Life forever
    Forever joy and peace
Our gain never
    Never lost or decreased
So I'm thanking
    Thanking God once again
Yes, I'm praising
    Praising God without end!

Pup in Arms

A young boy was once placed in foster care
At two he had been found with broken nose
Cigarette burns on his legs, a blank stare
Why from his grandfather, God only knows

One day at five this small boy came alive
Chancing upon a puppy in a cage
The boy raced to pet, for fear of neglect
Said, "I'm here for you." with love beyond age

Like a guide out of death's frost and darkness
A vital link between one lost and found
That little pup led a boy to gladness
Licks and laughter setting free what was bound

With pup in arms like love of the Shepherd
Child reborn now trusts with little effort

Holy Volition

A cathode ray opium tube
    A drug to dull the pain
A soporiferous false god
    Minimizing our gain
Spiritual alienation
    Emptiness and longing
Lost in waves of picture and sound
    Counterfeit belonging

Easily drawn into its web
    Where senses are rendered
Indifferent and unaware
    While souls are surrendered
Driven by an unconscious voice:
    "Seek escape from what's real
Just view the picture of your choice
    And transcend what you feel."

False absolutes can cause stupors
    Diminishing attempts
To receive and send true pictures
    Turn off that 'lectric hemp!
Talk to each other 'bout your pangs
    Receive God's transmission
There's power to live real, full lives
    With holy volition!

Cataclysmic Party Prep

There's a strange upheaval underway
Of muck and clutter and disarray
Like a faithful homemaker in spring
Christ is turning over everything!

Opening all the windows and doors
He's cleaning the soul ceiling to floor
Glad invitation to you and me
Let's party at your house demon free!

Christmas Dinner

There's an elephant at the table
As they pray grace for Christmas dinner
Bigger than life yet are they able
To see a truth that outweighs them all?

Silent they sit eyes closed to the pain
Hearts broken like the back of a chair
They lean on hope cautiously again
And pray that God's grace will be enough

Memories of that day in the fall
Send chills up the children's little spines
Mom and drunken dad had hit the wall
All the kids were whisked off to Grandma's

Dad was crying like a little boy
Mom was trying to be the adult
Off they went feeling scared, down and soiled
Leaving their dad to fend for himself

. . .

. . .
But the worst was still in the making
Dad's self-pity turned to a frightening rage
His roar left the neighbors shaking
As they watched him throw things out the door.

First the dishes then the pots and pans
Then flew their large dining room table
Smashing the plaster with his bare hands
Sending the chairs out into a heap

The pain of shame upon their return!
Their lives now just broken furniture
In a pile like kindling to be burned
Yet, not one word was ever spoken

Now a bump where the hole's re-plastered
An empty chair, its back broken out
An elephant still to be mastered
And a family with heads bowed in prayer

Is the host for the dinner missing?
No, He's the one painting this picture
Do you see what He's preparing?
Yes, it is beginning now to show

Amidst the ham, applesauce and peas
Baby's toy elephant lies
The wild animal's down on its knees
A new king's in charge of the jungle

Emmanuel outweighs elephants
They are no match to His great power
Be still, child, and see God triumphant
Praise! Rejoice! This is your Christmas feast!

Wedding Gift

In the heart of a double-breasted passion
Two young wonders made a brash break away
Fleeing from their first known pain and ashes
They set their sights on a new interplay

Did they know their wounded child went with them
Their greatest gift would be surprise rebirth?
That mere heat would not form their precious gem
Nor sheer will flame the fire of their self-worth?

Golden daisies and sweet white baby's breath
Loose-ringed promises on hopeful hearts
In time they'd find that real life stems from death
This Spirit-led link a kingdom growth art

With their two made one all else was undone
Now to travel past the end of the road
Love restored and freed each child to become
More fully graced by their heavenly code

Marital Dawn of Men and Women

Like a flash of lightning she flew through the kitchen
        An overachieving child with wet mop
In the hands of a grown woman's body

Her sharp tongue sounds off as in sibling rivalry
        Acting out as to prove herself worthy
To earn her place in house, home and family

Caught in the crossfire is a timid, little boy
        Feeling overwhelmed, shamed and belittled
Trying to lend the hand of a grown man

His first thoughts, "I must be bad. So, go now and hide."
        Acting out as to prove this thought worthy
He yields his place in house, home and family

Ah, but who shines into the depths of newlyweds
        Out from the mighty shadows of their fear?
Someone who stirs them to take heart and stand
            'Tis God's risen child, humanity's dear!

Meeting desperate little girls in their fight for rights
        With a loving, disarming presence that
Affirms their place among gracious, grown males

And sending scared boys out from their hiding
        With a truth that secures and reassures
Their place where kind, mature women prevail

So goes the marital dawn of men and women
        When loved and appreciated they rise
Sure, able, and creatively aligned
        A resurrection surprise!

Embryo Maker

Were hurt from previous heartache
Be sole source from which to proceed
Small chance would ever be taken
Few dreams would we ever conceive

How many a life has been lost
For fear of what living may cost?
What little discovery be
If trouble is all that's foreseen?

Yes, yes, this is certainly true
Yet, what, pray tell, of the stillborn
That horrible shock wave of blue
That pierces the heart
Takes our beat off the chart
And destroys the will through and through?

As in birth so in death a gasp
For breath that will start something new
Behind every endeavor lies
Forever a promise bestrewn

Be real or mere threat of stillborn
Mild or severe fear of hopes torn
The embryo maker knows strife
And delivers past sight—whole-life!

His Holy Break

Heavy on the peddle
    Light on common sense
Strong the urge to travel
    Weak from ego's wrench

Downhill from father's death
    Uphill bout for self
Young heart's need for love's breath
    Old genes steal mom's health

Manic goes grandiose
    Depressed draws drinks
Hungry for win to boast
    Fed a lie that stinks

Drifting out of control
    Stuck in self-pity
Vague like sight of a mole
    Clear anxiety
. . .

. . .
Off he goes with peaches
    On the floor for brakes
Fresh fruit never reaches
    Spoiled by dreadful stakes

Rough skinned yield hits the wall
    Smooth sailing life smashed
Freestone fruit takes a fall
    Clingstone flesh torn, bashed

Dark moth leaves legacy
    Light twig nipped in the bud
All innocence at sea
    None found free of mud

Dim the mirror of grace
    Bright the Son of God
Lost sweet taste by the case
    Found before the sod

Frowns spawn by his disgrace
    Smiles for the child's sake
Sin is the loser's place
    Saint his holy break

Surefooted Grace

Two figures on
Top a ladder
Striving to climb unto proof
Child at bottom
No slight matter
Seizing the rungs like a tollbooth

A worst nightmare
Ladder toppling
Try as he may to hold it firm
Oh, what a fright
Mom, Dad squirming
As backwards they plunge disconfirmed!

Did he fall short?
Is this his fault?
No, he could not hold them upwards
Two grown adults
Still same results
Septic shame's like falling backwards

Fears face the past
Not where we are
But they guide the chide toward the truth
Jacob's ladder
A falling star
On surefooted grace rise, be soothed!

Case of Empty Promises

All eyes were on dad as he stood by the kitchen sink
    Our hearts longed to trust him when he said he wouldn't drink
"I quit! No more! Do you believe what I am saying?"
    We believed but was unbelief that kept us praying
One bottle after another he dumped down the drain
    A case of empty promises and just wasted pain?
Were we deceived to think our lives could be something more?
    No, Lord, let this be that new day we've been waiting for!

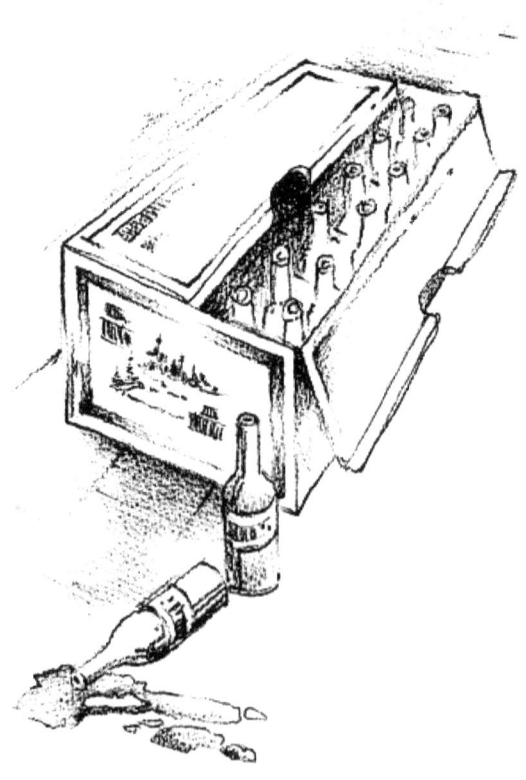

Oh, silly me, to think dad could keep his promises
    And what's to become of us as his word regresses?
Another case of beer's been delivered to our door
    Seems he's right back drinking just like he did before
Please tell me! Where is the truth so I can understand?
    I feel like a helpless child in never-never land.
I quit! No more! I can't believe what he is saying.
    Yet, in spite of unbelief, Lord, I keep on praying!

That my faith in You will lead me to recovery
    That reasons for hope will be daily discoveries
That I'll find Your Word is truth and always trustworthy
    That my life today need not be so topsy-turvy
That there's freedom from the shame of my earthly father
    That the way beyond addiction is worth the bother
That with Christ I stand erect in all of my sorrow
    That no empty promises will spoil my tomorrow

Red Pop

How much did it cost to
    Buy his son strawberry pop?
And how much did dad drink
    Before he finally stopped?

Off they went to the park
    Or so the trusting son thought
But the bar was as far
    The little boy ever got

The park with his son or
    Had he planned this all along?
Lord only knows dad's thoughts
    But they both knew this was wrong

"What pop for you, son?
    You can have any you'd like."
"I'll try that red kind, Dad."
    Wishing for home and his bike

Drink stirred up emotion
    Drunk and stinking with defeat
Dad drove wildly back home
    His son scared white as a sheet

There was pop on his lips
    And his dad's angry red face
But was mom's disgust that
    Left him alone and disgraced

Was he of more value
    Than a bottle of red pop?
He wasn't really sure
    Because it cost him a lot

Strong in the Song

I will chance the dance beyond what's normal
And will follow God's lead from start to end
Why stand in a lie before truth's portal
When I can prance with my Savior and friend?

Choose a masquerade and steal what is real?
What satisfaction is there in dying?
My life has problems 'bout which God deals
My joy more in being than in trying

That ground of my being—a second birth
From snowstorm reborn in warm, wet font
I prune to God's tune for healthy self-worth
Free to heal and feel and voice what I want!

Alive I will thrive in step with the Lord
No loss will now toss me topsy-turvy
Strong in the song of one saving accord
No blast from my past able to stop me!

Wholly Begotten!

Siblings—all of us
Some travel off
Others remain
All feel distant
In our search for home

Some like the young one are
Wild shooting stars
Spirit tumbleweeds
Blind jaywalkers
Bolting for freedom

Others like first born
Are lights gone dark
Increasingly mad
Iron edgy
Stuck in what's righteous

What's this condition
Near or away
Dutiful, rash
Gasping for breath
Fighting for a niche

Entangled, confused
So out of sorts
Where human heart
Mind and spirit
Simply come up short?

It's divine drama
Soul-gestation
Maturation
Predictable
Pangs of second birth!

Dressed in vain effort
Prone to despair
We can feel trapped
And exposed to
Painful emptiness

Yet, lost not alone
Senses, awake!
Hardships can be
Pathways to peace
Trust and be drawn home!

To that glorious
Figure of grace
Who made you and
Raised you and who'll
Gift you with shalom

What a wonder this
Prodigal Star
Who shines when we
Fall dim and who
Warms when we grow cold
. . .

. . .
What a surprise to
Reach this milestone
Mercy covered
Greeted with a
Sweet homecoming kiss!

What a joy to be
Ringed with One who
Throws love parties
Each of us prized
Forever God's own!

Still there are loved ones
Searching for roots
Seeking the sun
To bear good fruit
Tend to this garden

Spiritual journey
Heavenly hosts
Grown, mature we
Welcome them home
All heirs—Imagine!

Come, Sacred Kingdom
Eden restored
Saintly parade
No one Ignored
Wholly begotten!

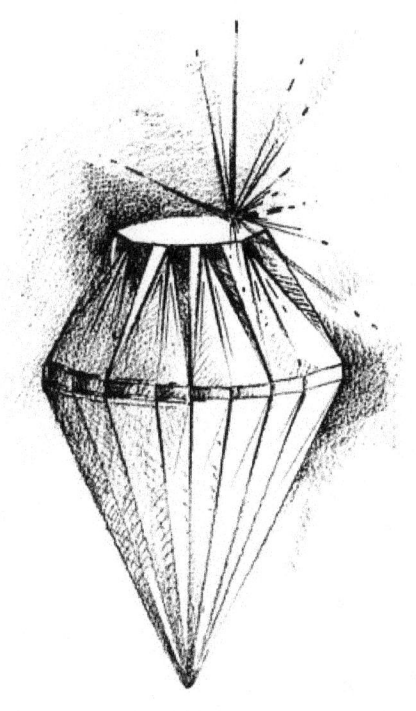

Diamonds

Just common graphite, pressure and heat
Yet, diamonds we know are tough to beat
Just basic elements, breath from sod
Yet, priceless one infant in the eyes of God!
Each human being a work of art
A life-long project from the start
No slapdash shortcuts or instant formation
Our whole is well beyond simple summation
Never far from the hand of the artist
Cross creativity stretched the farthest
Birth pang of deadly volcanic feat
Life is God's gift
But we don't
come
cheap!

Joy-o-meter

What is your number today? You ask.
Like wanting to know the pressure of
The atmosphere for flight of the dove
Or seeing past my attitude's mask

If I say, "I'm a one, two or three."
Does this mean I am less than human?
That my soul has seeped into the sand?
Mere doom and gloom is all there will be?

What if I am a four, five or six?
Am I just a stationary front?
Not dead or alive but in the hunt
For catalytic joypop's quick fix

How about a seven or an eight?
Does the height of my mood paint the sun?
Tell realistic expectations?
Will that moment's pleasure seal my fate?

Forget the illusive nine or ten
Lord only knows what that must be like!
This troubled world where faith has to fight
Will keep me wondering to the end

So do not ask me, "What's my number?"
I simply can't give a true reading
But go with me where God is leading
Joyance measured by blood on lumber

Just Grateful

Designer of the dawn
    Painter par excellence
How might I thank you
    nearly enough?

You, my lavish giver
    Delighting every sense
I undeserving
    Just busted stuff

Still you paint a picture
    New of me each day
Life-sign unfolding
    Grace in the rough

How I pray that others
    See you gladly at work
Art of creation
    Not useless fluff

The beauty of the dawn
    Your promise each new day
Purposeful living
    Not off the cuff

Grand artist of all life
    Paint me as you desire
But I just grateful?
    Yes, that's enough!

REFLECTION/DISCUSSION QUESTIONS

1. Who knows the way you are looking to go in your life?
2. What's the difference between an inner and an outer journey?
3. What do feelings have to do with your journey through life?
4. How do you experience shame? What does it look like? How does it feel?
5. Is there such a thing as good shame?
6. What are some shadows in your life? Are such shadows dangerous? Why? Why not?
7. Think of a time when you became emotionally numb. Was there a "winter thaw"? How did that come about?
8. How comfortable is your "inner child" usually? How do you help your child feel safe to play?
9. What memory from childhood validates and affirms your worth as a person?
10. At home where is your "mercy seat"?
11. Ever feel like you're caught in a "tug of war" between good and evil? How do you respond? What helps?
12. How might gratitude contribute to one's validity?

Discovery

Stirred by the Spirit of God and our soul's search for her essence, the ordinary stuff of life lights up in a sacred spectrum of sensual grace, insight and wonder.

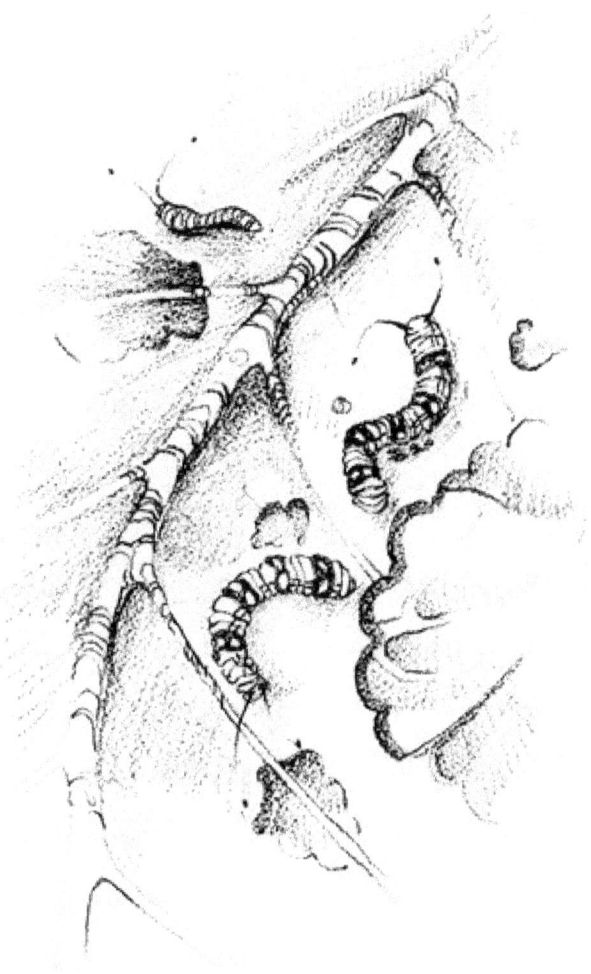

Beckoning

Pillars of billowing white steam
      Rise above Goose Lake
This early summer morn

Indeed, one of Minnesota's
      Enchanting moments
This new day now adorned!

In silk clouds over calm water
      Senses play witness
To God's Spirit moving

Ears perk up to sweet beckoning:
      "Come, my precious one.
Enter this day's dawning.
      Enjoy my grace and glory!"

Catch the Wonder

Catch the wonder of life around you
    Enjoy the grace God affords
See with eyes now opened wide
    Breathe deep the breath of life
For the secret of seeing is setting the sail
    And feeling God's Spirit blow free

Catch the wonder of life around you
    Hear God speak to you now
Through Word and nature God sings a love song
    Uniting hearts as one
For the secret of hearing is giving an ear
    To the song and whisper of God

Lord of order and space, matter, time, human race
    Shape our lives, fill us now with delight
Grant us faith, make us new, awake our senses to you
    Help us all gain heavenly sight
And though our visions of wonder come and they go
    May you and your love still abide

Catch the wonder of life around you
    Taste the goodness of God
Bread and wine poured out in plenty
    Granting us all new life
For the secret of hunger is feeding the soul
    And letting God's cup overflow

Catch the wonder of life around you
    Reach out and touch someone
As you tend to one who is needful
    You'll find God touching you
For the secret of feeling the presence of God
    Is letting God's love flow through you

Catch the wonder of life. It's the pearl of great price
    It's a gift. A total surprise!
Let my eyes dance with glee. Let my tongue sing of Thee.
    Let your love shine through me clear and bright
And though our visions of wonder come and they go
    May you and your love still abide

God's Smile

Bask in God's being
And find our own in the midst
Bask in graced seeing
And note valued existence
Bask in God's wooing
And discover life's purpose
Bask in graced doing
And spot God smiling at us!

In My Mist

There is mystery in my makeup
Majesty in my mist
There is nothing that is certain
Save that something
Three has kissed
Made in love
Bought through sorrow
New day dawns
Bright tomorrow
Calm comes before clarity
Fact gives way to faith
Mind gives up the chase
In my mist
i am known
Glimmer turns to glow
Light grows brighter
Sacred sparkle
Soul delight
Mystery
Majesty

I Am
Magnified!

Clouds over my Head

Clouds over my head
   Is God dead?

  Just a figment of
     Imagination
        A yearning for love
           In cloud formation?

             See Almighty God
                In people, places, things!
                    Scenes where nature nods
                        Buildings where bells ring!

Clouds over my head
   Pillar lead

  Billowy way home
     Floating face of grace
       Never leaves alone
         Guides the human race

             Vapor from on high
                Spark of earth and wing
                    Wind in word and wine
                       Livens everything!

Clouds over my head
   Soul is fed

         Moving constantly
         Can you see?

Gooey Ducks

Ever meet a duck
    Hiding in the sand?
In bubbling muck
    You'll find these strange clams

Harvested for meat
    Roasted on the beach
Down in a heartbeat
    A delicacy!

Ever made to feel
    Stuck deep in a can
While some wheel and deal
    Happy as a clam?

Don't be fooled by mere
    Two-shelled, bi-valued freaks
Rise up! Do not fear!
    Taste the life you meet!

Hopper in the Grass

Hopper in the grass
Caleb with giants
Feeling like a bug
In a world of self-reliance

Look what lies ahead
Spies note obstacles
Can't begin to grow
With fear-filled heart and vessels

But…
Can't grass become bread?
And blood become wine?
Can't impossible
Become possible
When will is divine?

Hoppers don't just hop
Giants don't just stomp
A worm can learn to fly
After just one stop!

So…
Go ahead, Caleb
With God fear fades
Go, Joshua, June
A new world awaits!

Pearl of Great Price

Notice your pain
    Feel your abscess
In that dark place
    God's mercies rinse

Not a scapegoat
    Nor enabler
Focus on the
    Great Creator

Trust Love's promise
    For your healing
In everything
    There is meaning

Speck in the flesh
    Thorn in side~ Your
Pearl of great price
    Birthed not denied

True Friendship

Who's our true, lasting friend?
    How do we know for sure?
That just beyond the bend
    Betrayal won't occur?

"I'm on your side," he said.
    I should have known better
That when the weak had fled
    'Twas like he'd not met her

True friendship's whom I mean
    Not just with me but Thee
To one with whom we're seen
    Grounded in deity

Author of all friendship
    Ours pale when we compare
Your love gives us a tip
    It's grace, not how we fare

Empowered by Your call
    We give our very best
Yet, subject to the fall
    It's You who'll pass the test

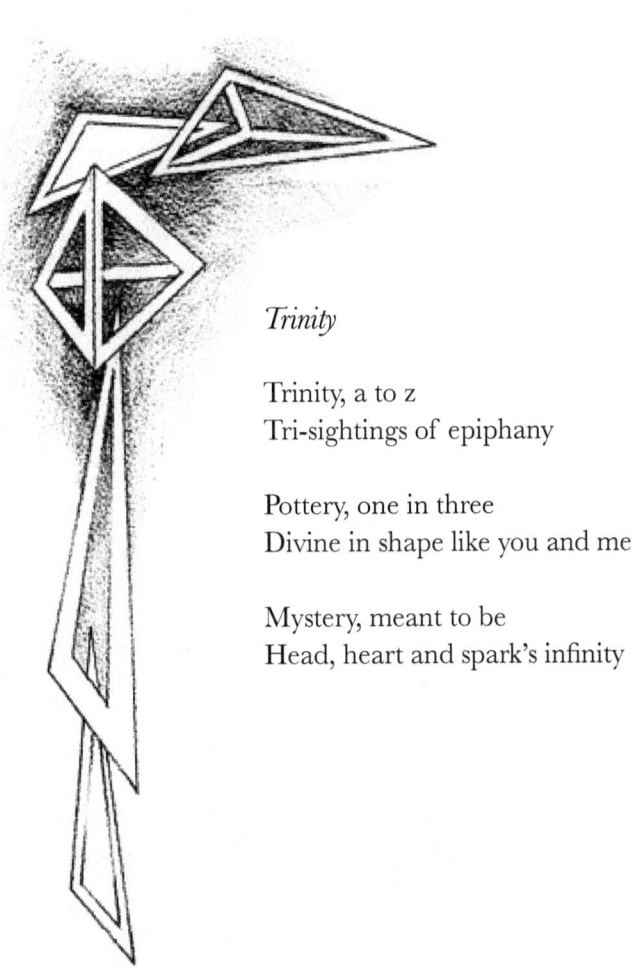

Trinity

Trinity, a to z
Tri-sightings of epiphany

Pottery, one in three
Divine in shape like you and me

Mystery, meant to be
Head, heart and spark's infinity

Born Again

Come, be born again
Chance life in open spaces
Your heart of hearts welcomes you
Where you can feel, taste and touch
The Spirit of life
Breathing freely without fear
True self arising
Quickened by the love of God

Seattle

Needle in the sky
    Music down below
Bright sails on the Sound
    Young heart wants to know

'Bout that big digger
    How deep will it go?
Driver in his seat
    How does he know?

And how does it move
    That sleek monorail?
High above the streets
    Smoother than a sail

Oh, sweet child in me
    Be my eye and ear
Make love for learning
    My life-long career

Mount Tallac

A cascade of stones on hills so steep
Dust with hot sun and shadowed earth with moist smells of death
Birds sing sweet songs while our muscles weep
Like whistling breeze through pine, you can hear us fetch our breath

Weather-worn white timbers point the way
Floating Island shines toward desired destiny
Blue and emerald lakes grant firm names
To terra incognita beyond a line of trees

Fallen Leaf, Half Moon, Cathedral Pool
Stir hearts and eager feet beside wild mountain flowers
Path hard with granite, a guiding jewel
Above the fluid of all living things where God towers

That bright, bold peak, though a grain of sand
Reflects a life swashed in sweaty red Olivet rain
Dazed at the might of the Savior's hand
And soothed by a brief, holy sight gained
Our miniscule mass of molecules is ordained

Choir of Waterfalls

Oh, choir of waterfalls
Sweet and majestic is your call
How you reflect life
And wet our appetite!
We at home in that sound
Of countless drops from glacier rim
Those bits of moisture
Flowing with good and bad
Life seemingly shattered by
Their brief fall
Yet by grace
Smooth and tranquil
In the end

Midnight Sun

Just above the Artic Circle
In the land of reindeer and trolls
Truth is told
Behold! Light of the Midnight Sun!

While dark in some earthly places
The sun always shines and faces
Toward truth
Our life in the light of God's grace

Duck Pond Dawn

Bright glow of the sun
    Over smooth waters
Sounds of nature call
    Awe never falters

The rise of Eden
    Past storms forgotten
Ducks dip deep, tail up
    Clouds look like cotton

Drop in vast oceans
    Yet straight to the heart
Life in one motion
    Glory Day's new start!

Bird Tale

Jackie Rueh was strong, tall and lank
An older friend across the street
Talkative and full of wild pranks
Seemed I'd run from trouble each time we'd meet

So, yes, I should have known better
When he told me how to catch birds
"Salt shaker's your best bet.
Spread some on their tails and you'll have them in herds."

Meant to impress like no other
I set off with salt shaker in hand
After one tail and another
Determined to net a pet with this grand plan

It might have been just ten minutes
But then maybe a full hour
Neighbors must have thought I was nuts
But it was at home my plan turned sour

"What you doin' with that shaker?"
My dad asked me in disbelief
"I'm bird huntin' long as it takes.
Just need some more salt and you're gonna see."

That wasn't the first or the last
Of the tricks played on me as a boy
But a life lesson learned stands fast
Chasing dreams is what I truly enjoy

Minnesota Lake Place

Loon dips deep in the early morn
    Like my spirit in this home
      When I visit

Fire burns warm, the air is quiet
    Like the peace of God's grace
      I love this place!

Dance at the Lake

It would have been plenty
    To be at the lake on
A beautiful sunny day

But then came the sunset
    Cool breeze, lightning bugs and
A twinkling star-lit night

And I like new dawn, glad
    Movements of thankfulness
Danced God's dance of pure delight!

Lovely Lambent Server

Crescent moon shines above a lucent-eyed mother
Beautiful union of heart, hand, faith and full cup
Content and not concerned about spilling over
With glimmering column of blue steam, she looks up

Mysterious, physical illusion have we?
Like ice crystals form snowflakes spontaneously
Where many millions of microscopic mirrors
Reflect a light source that can chase away life's drear?

This bright colored sight on a dark December morn
Is no shiv'ring lost child in a cold sea of fright
'Tis sweet sign of the pure love from which we are born
Cup of blessing delivered for the world's delight!

Pregnant dawn at its best lived one day at a time
Come sup from the cup that tastes of glory divine!
Our souls in the sparkling starlight of God's promise
Oh, lovely lambent server, your child's among us!

Sight of re-creation cupped in holy silence
Eastward light sensation, vast God's sacred presence
Love's warm blood flowing, within and beyond the rim
Great day in the morning! Be gone dark world of sin!

Sacred Walking

Oh, lordly labyrinth landscape
      Sure morning-star navigation
Faith's eye view for a bold escape
      From this upside-down creation

Cartographic revolution
      Passed body, mind and lost spirit
A field of dream constellations
      Anxiety cast from orbit

Sacred walking transportation
      Shapes the world so differently!
Centered spiritualization
      Prayer-lit path to boon liberty

From river bend, flagpole, stone church
      God's eye map leads voyagers on
Bypass toll plazas while in search
      For that home where hearts belong

This and More

Invited to meet full reality
    By that one profound, ground of being
Disclosed through faith and all fields of science
    An obvious "this" in our space-time world
And that magnanimous, stupendous "more"

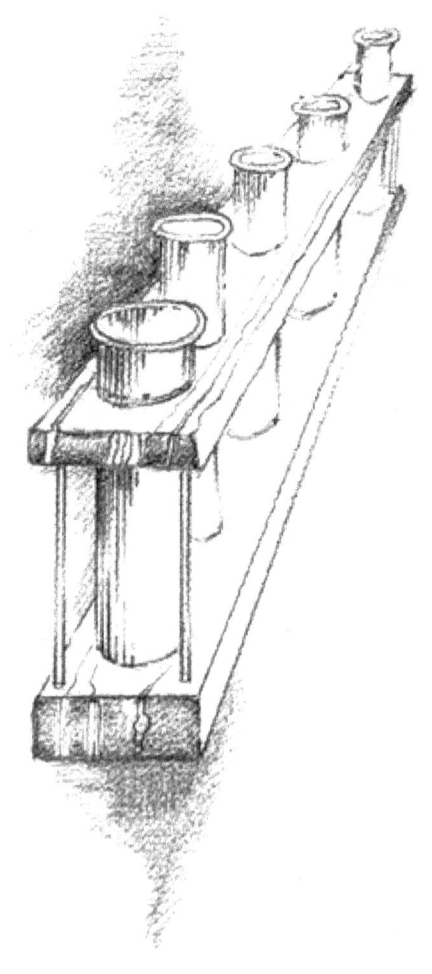

State to State

Waves of grain bow
To state's greater extent
But for the wind on her North Shore
'Tis the fresh sound of Lake Superior

Mighty the wheat
Feeding mouths of millions
Mightier still, those soothing waves
That break on the shore of every womb

Creator, God
You to whom all things bow
Let your Spirit blow life into
Our bread and water, state to state, endless

Better Beauty

Reflections of God
    In creation's carriage
Warmth of divine heart
    In the sweetest marriage

Yet better than these
    Is the grace God is pleased
To bestow on lowly
    Ones such as me

Tunneling

Against the rockiest of rock
    The slipperiest of sloops
Through snow-capped mountains
    Under wild Billy goats
A tunnel is burrowed
    A sure hope realized
As human effort meets God's grace
    And life shines from the other side!

By our own strength and pace
    We'd just dig a deeper hole
But with God's tools in place
    We are sure to reach our goal
That bright light through subways
    Our first sight of paradise
Where fresh water flows, fruit trees grow
    And life opens up deep and wide!

Clear as Broad Daylight

The deep drum of eternity
    Sounds forth wise within me
Yet, blind eyes can not see

Clamors of chaos surround me
    Still voice gently soothes me
Soul stirs expectantly

How might I tell of such a life
    That lies on strange land heights
Far from the world's dark might?

'Tis secret word that blossoms bright
    In ears' wide open sight
Now clear as broad daylight

Frost

Gray templed earth
Glistens in the still of an early morning sun
Golden arms and bright red fingers
Embrace a bargaining heart
Eyes lifted heavenward while
Veto and nettle fall like leaves from timber
Vigorous fowl spell victory in the cool, open air
And alas, I warmly welcome the sights and sounds of the season's end

Wonderful Names
Wondrous Lord!

God is our Maker
By grace I am who I am
Folly, self-made man!

Wind over waters
Oh, life-giving breath of God
Come and spirit me

Glory and my shield
Be lifter up of my head
Heart of all worship

Seed of the Woman
From bosom of the Father
Rise to shade my sin!

Significant Sign
Born God in lowly manger
That we understand

Better day promised
Far beyond this troubled world
Our Star now shinning

Shepherd of souls
Bring back your precious lambs for
Your name's sake, Amen!

Let all now enter
High Tower from enemies
In you we are safe

Strong Rock of refuge
Our firm foundation for faith
Stone atoning grace

Oh, precious Manna
Cast new vigor on our souls
Feed us your essence

Shadow from the heat
Cool beyond all conception
Relief for weary

How great our longing
Live Water in dry places
Quench our thirsty souls!

Right use of knowledge
In you oh, precious Wisdom,
We do will of God

Hope of God's people
Stirs us to will and to do
For sake of the world

Let the Blood now flow
In the heart of every soul
Your cross not in vain

Oh, Everlasting!
Age-abiding is our God
Changeless, perfect, Thee!

Reflection/Discussion Questions

1. Have you ever felt the presence of God in nature? When? Where? What was it like?

2. Have you ever felt like God was smiling at you? When? Where? What was it like?

3. What lessons in life have you learned from nature and wildlife?

4. How have seasons enriched your life?

5. Where do you go and what do you do outside your home to experience a sense of the sacred?

6. Do you find the sacred or does the sacred find you?

7. Who are the people who help you discover God in your life?

8. What can you give up to embrace more of the sacred in your daily life?

9. How do you experience the sacred in your work? Who are you working for?

10. If you could experience the sacred in your life in one new way what might it be?

11. What names drawn from nature do you use to describe God?

12. Do you hear the sacred calling? When? Where?

Community

When community is built on dreams alone we are likely to be overcome by disillusionment. A faith community is grounded in divine reality. The essence of this community is light and love in which we are invited to participate.

Community

A miracle is taking place
Do you have eyes to see it?
Is your heart ready to receive it?
Today we can celebrate our similarities
Today we can embrace what divides
Today we can feel the smooth skin of shalom
For God has fathered a child called Trust
And we have the honor of birthing Him
Yes, we have the joy
And we have the challenge
Of raising community
Unto full maturity!

Welcome to the Neighborhood!

God is our community
    Father, Spirit and the Son
Multi-countenance we see
    Like the church many and one

We the people are the church
    All one body in the Lord
Growing, caring while we search
    For shalom that grace affords

Yes, God's house is dear to us
    Creed and practice grant us strength
Yet, it is God's love we trust
    Lifts and carries us full length

And the races plenty be
    Made in God's diversity
God unequivocally good
    Welcome to the neighborhood!

Raising Up Fun

Come join, sweet child, now of age this circle
Where favor is found in playing a fool
Normal you're not in shell of a turtle
Align with light-hearted, you precious jew'l

What risks disapproval you coming out?
Silly won't mock problems not really yours
Fellowship of laughter, smiles all about
Grave one, raise fun! Break from behind those doors

We'll lift the lid off past chronic trauma
Feed your glad soul with deep glee day by day
Playable, freed from serious stigma
You'll recover your child . . . Please come our way!

To this a broad circle of faith, humor
Where joy is stirred in hearts of late bloomers

Leader Led

Is it the leader who leads or
    What leads the leader
That stirs God's people
    To chance their next faithful step?

Both provide essentials called for
    Soul that remembers
Human potential
    And God's vast power for pep

Mountains moved without their knowing
    Small change too proves true
Chieftain led to try
    Believing God's grace will come through

Shepherds are the shift they're leading
    Trust in heart made new
Steering self to die
    That shalom be seen in clear view

Hallowed Mission Statement

See boldly written on the temple wall
A household god protecting one and all
Grandiosity or bold faith, we choose
But what's seen as true, suggests most will loose

A stated goal can become a quick fix
Unimpressive records reveal its tricks
Hooked on a promise with no thought to how
We're conned by homage to a golden cow

With the intent to unite in one voice
We fall prey to this hallowed drug of choice

God's Gift of Community

How I loved my dreams of Christian fellowship
    More than community in Christ itself!
So, by God's right my precious dreams were stripped
    Shattered were my plans for God, others and self

Good thing since wish dreams can be worst enemies
    And I but fail what we need and desire most
By sheer grace God has not granted all my schemes
    But upends my hope to unite lest I boast

For the church is not a human endeavor
    But a divine, spiritual reality
God's Word and deed are what bind us forever
    One together in Christ's saving love are we

Now, as I enter God's gift of community, say
    Not demander but thankful recipient
I watch the morning mists of my dreams give way
    To the dawn of that fellowship God has sent

Living in the Tension

Longing for the ideal
Criticizing the real
Rap becomes a problem
Settling for the real
Not striving for ideal
Laps life from all of them

Amazing points of view
A mix of old and new
Tap possibilities
Some may disappoint you
But none need destroy you
Apt grace the guarantee

Maturity is won
When rigid is undone
Cap is off the tension
Expectations are fun
Grounded you reach for sun
Map for resurrection!

Miracle on the Hill

Miracle on a Seattle hill
Angels deliver a heartthrob thrill
Long the labor well worth the clear risk
Child is born, majesty in her mist

To be with love always is her name
Honor God and warm hearts why she came
A light on the rise from the first day
Gift that keeps shining all of life's way

Delightful child, wonderful trav'ler
From hill to the plain and hereafter
Growing in years, in wisdom and grace
Girl now a mother in her own place

Raising her young with heart, mind and soul
Two precious boys, God's prize to make whole
Grateful for firstborn daughter and friend
Grant from on high from start to the end

And as though this dole were not enough
A second child was given to us!
We praise the Giver of all good things
Especially for children hearts now sing

Yes, a tall order raising a child
No easy rules for mild or for wild
Yet, that One who gives them to us all
Protects and gently leads large and small

Thrills and Chills

It's not suppose to snow that late
    Total white out, thirteen inches
On the fourteen of April!

It's not suppose to take this long
    Drawn out labor, a few inches
And just a mere seven pounds!

It's not suppose to be this fun
    To find delight so easily
Her laugh, smile, engaging style!

It's not suppose to be this hard
    Raising a child, eighteen plus years
When we love each other so

It's not suppose to cause us pain
    Cutting the cord, launching a child
When we know it goes this way

But what if we knew in the end
    It's okay not to worry
(Unless we choose to worry)

What if we knew our worst of fears
    Will work out well, that what's happened
Transpired in our best interest?

What if we were all guaranteed
    Those we love, will have what they need
To be whom they're meant to be?

What if we knew our future's good
    Working its way out as it should
Secure in the arms of grace?

Surely we'd celebrate today
    That our child was born in a storm
That we've been blessed to enjoy
    The thrills
        and chills
            of parenting!

Lost No More

Travel on winding roads
Living a harried life
Sheep often show up lost
And we're faced with a choice
Ignore and chase away
Or embrace and show love?

W.W.J.D. you ask?
Yes, what would Jesus do?
Slow and show compassion
That is a certainty
But is this possible
With lost like you and me?

If what we're told is true
A little faith will do
Life's learning how to love
Help comes from God above
To reach the way we're shown
Arriving safe at home

Claim It and Act!

When you discover something
That's a gift from God.
Don't let it be labeled odd.
    Claim it!

Some won't know what's important
Miss the deepest part
So, dear to you from the start
    Claim it!

Yours a solid inner base
Where you speak and track.
Against all that may attack
    Claim it!

Follow your artful drawing.
No call is too small.
Oh, wonder child, have a ball!
    Claim it!

All you gifted from on high
Let nothing detract.
Humbly and convincingly
    Claim it and act!

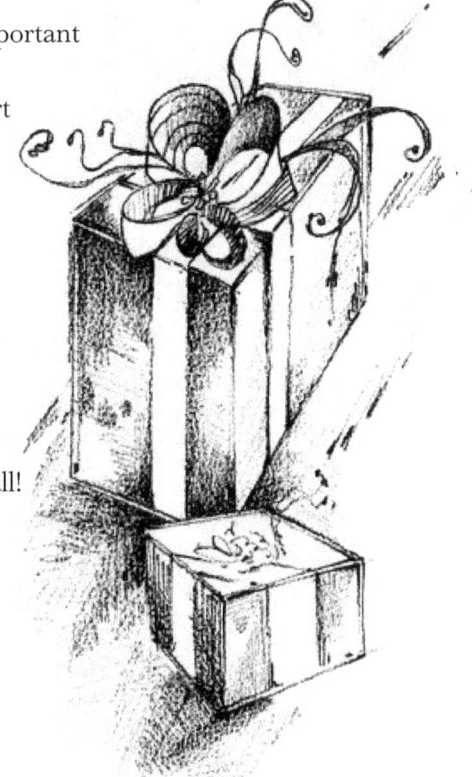

Ticket to Significance

From the El Dorados
    To the Butterscotch Grove
We were a band of school kids
    On a treasure hunt for gold

We played simple chord runs
    Sang rough harmonies and
Even won a contest once
    On a Quad Cities TV

Dreaming of the lime light
    Gathering more equipment
Play became more serious
    And out on the road we went

It was the sixties then
    And things began to fly
In a psychedelic bus
    We'd have made our mothers cry

Where were we all going?
    Weren't we meant to be stars?
Yet that bus rode in circles
    And we never got too far

Then I quit the Grove band
    No, music hadn't died
Though it was plenty scary
    To think I had lost my ride

Those friends had been my life
    We'd grown from boys to men
We'd made a name for ourselves
    Rock music our medium

But true love grabbed my heart
    Creating a new song
Though old tunes did die hard
    I soon learned where I belong

While the band helped me cope
    Protecting me for years
I would have missed my true call
    For only blood, sweat and tears

From bus to a soul train
    I traveled to new birth
Then on wings of an airplane
    I flew high onto self-worth

One true music maker
    Gives all bands a quick glance
But hearts that beat for God net
    Tickets to significance

My Caribou

Spin of the grinder and
Rattle of coffee beans
Music overhead and
Fun voices all around

A social connection
Or the buzz of caffeine?
Whatever the reason
Seems he does like this spot

Though preferring quiet
He visits here often
To read and to ponder
And write a quick poem

My Caribou? It's a place
For gregarious reindeer
Where cups of fun overflow
And human souls stop to rear
Good cheer here and to go

Headed for Bodø

Many on the move
One on two smooth groves
It's an all-day journey from Tronheim
But few seem to mind
Headed for Bodø

Truth our voices sent
We are different
Yet all breathe the air of adventure
Locals and foreign
Headed for Bodø

Beauty meets the eye
Tree, water and sky
Hills and valleys stirring the senses
Paradise revealed
Headed for Bodø

Bread, cheese and apples
Food for the travels
Foretaste of a meal we'll share when we
Hunger, thirst no more
Headed for Bodø

. . .

. . .
Ride, purposeful fun
Roll inspiration
Meet meaning on this appointed day
Rainbow in one ray
Headed for Bodø

Steer this row of steal
Control every wheel
All we just trust the one who leads us
Blind faith stays the course
Headed for Bodø

Destiny is won!
Midnight summer sun
Preview of a time that's coming
When light drowns darkness
Three cheers for Bodø!

Visit to Røsvik

There was a geranium in the window
and sunlight from above
shining through a house soaked in sorrow
yet filled with love.
Yes, cold was the story
we heard from our host
about the death of her father
in a storm off the coast.
Eighteen Norwegian fishermen
He was captain of the boat
Seventeen died
Just one stayed afloat
All of Røsvik mourned
this tragic loss of life.
But one rose quickly~
The captain's wife

. . .

. . .
She had home and a business
that needed to be run.
So by a strength from within
and help from her people,
she set sights on grieving forward
and . . . pressed on.
Tears welled up
when we remarked of her mother's courage.
Then sorrow gave way
to grace once again.
From old family pictures
hung on a wall
we glanced through the window
to spring flowers standing tall.
And just beyond a field of green
stood a little church steeple
that stirred faith in our hearts
and joy for these people.

Human Race

Got a package the other day
From a place not too far away
In it was a bright gold medal
Results of a contest settled

Beginning late in that short race
I set out on a steady pace
Before long I'd gone the distance
Overcoming all resistance

Giving my full name at the end
Never a thought that I might win
Many others had gone ahead
But I'd kept my pace Spirit-led

Now to receive this winner's prize
I am most certainly surprised
Yet, I see in little black print
What answers this predicament

My life's hike to the finish line
Is fixed by God's graceful design
In Christ we win the human race
With a grand prize for all—first place!

Campfire

Warmth and glow of a campfire seize the night
    Songs and laughter lift people circled tight
There young and old we gather with I Am
    The ghosts of this world bow to the Lamb
Near shore under star-studded skies we see
    Faith fired up, souls saved, all creation now
        God's community!

Hospital Calls

Third kind of cancer
Attacking her body
Young man struggling
With the loss of his leg
Old man wondering
If he'll live 'til tomorrow
Where's the Lord's light today
In the din of these rounds?

Ah, yes, there's the child
Delighting the crowd
The nurse with a smile
A kind man in a gown
The lift of laughter
On an elevator ride
Cheerful voice from above
Small joys and simple love

These you see the Savior
Warm heart of the divine
Holy angels in charge
Roll call to Easter life
God's sure voice from above
For times that get stone tough
When little to do or say
Thanks Lord for lightened way!

Christ's Heart

To know something is one thing
      To use what we know is quite another
To love someone is something
      To love like God loves is like no other
To help someone's a good thing
      To serve as unto the Lord is better
To pardon is a God thing
      Forgive our self is a matching letter
It's smart to live for something
      Christ's heart to give our life for those hard pressed
There's joy living the good life
      Great joy giving away the very best!

God So Loves Them!

Two hearts overflow in one loving theme
      A handsome bride and groom by God's decree
Amazing grace glistens from these two gems
      Yes, we can see how our God so loves them!

Come gird your sharp sword oh, most holy Lord
      Protect these and theirs from harm on all shores
Steadfast defense shine bright as high noon
      That they and we too may surely love you

Oh, God, our sweet bliss, bless them with gladness
      Grace them secure for both joy and sadness
Lead them along in earthly vocation
      Perfect their love for heavenly station

We see your grace now shine forth from this place
      Your love made so real for whole human race
Bless our endeavors, from us not sever
      That we may praise and thank you forever!

Two hearts overflow in one loving theme
      This handsome assembly by God's decree
Amazing grace glistens from these two gems
      That 'bout us be said, "How God so loves them!"

Crows on a Crossbeam

A crow circles and lands
On a crossbeam
Towering above the
House of the Lord
The sight draws fright.
What on earth does this mean?
A sign of defiance
Or one accord?

Now a second bird lands
Across from first
The two held up on both
Arms of the cross
Fright takes flight
No longer thinking the worst
Since all perched on Christ rise
High 'bove their loss

Pentecostal Delight

Whop the drums, wham the hands!
    Lift our voices as high as we can!
Dance in the aisles freestyle
    Praise outlasts strong arms of the clock dial

Stir up the fever of
    God's spark, fanning to flames the white dove
Burn, baby, burn purified!
    Not a one of us will be denied

Bow our knees, own one's sin
    Then get right up on our feet again
Oh, sup the goodness of the Lord
    In this doting service no one is bored!

A Good Boat

Lord, you have helped us build a good boat
Why don't we set sail?
The wind is still blowing
The star is still glowing
Don't let us stay in the harbor

Spirit-led soul search
"Son-shine" in the dark
Travel through danger
Solar vessel riding the waves

Symbol of voyage
Way for those living
Cross for the dead
Ah, but what about those dark storms?

What if we get lost?
What if the goods run out?
What if the waves beat strong?
What if our hearts grow weak and cold?

Haunted waterways
Perils of the world
Powers of the passions
We are afraid of the very worst

Lord, you have helped us build a good boat
Never meant for harbor
Built for open waters
How our faith totters!
Wind picks up and we down the sail

Faithful, Ferryman, isn't your tow secure?
Holy, Pilot, isn't your way now made sure?
Tell, creative Navigator
Designer of the boat
Isn't bold faith born in a storm?

Mighty beginnings
Potent to the end
Toward whole and home
In the pitch of intensity

Oh, storm-tossed vessel
Precious Noah's Ark
Courage in promise
This ship will not sink!

Lord, you have helped us build a good boat
Passengers await
Free us from the fear of sailing
Free us from the fear of failing
Let us go in faith!

A Fresh New Start

You've cleared our vision
You've stirred our hearts
You've healed division
A fresh new start!

We feel the difference
We see the change
We taste the goodness
Life's not the same

We share your glory
We know your grace
We tell your story
Love face to face

Reflection/Discussion Questions

1. What contributes to a soulful community?

2. What communities do you belong to that feed your soul?

3. How do you contribute to the communities in which you belong?

4. How does being created in the image of God contribute to your relationship with others?

5. Do you naturally have fun or do you need the help of others?

6. Where does tension lie in your life? Does any of this tension serve a good purpose?

7. What small group has served to offer you support from which you have grown?

8. What favorite public place has delighted your senses and helped you connect with others?

9. In what faith "boat" do you travel?

10. How do you balance time together with others and time alone?

11. Who are your steadfast friends?

12. Can you have too many brothers and sisters in the faith community?

Futurity

The future faith reveals is not one of shadowy deprivation but fullness, joy and abundance. Like the rising sun at the dawn of a new day, we are invited to walk into it and see for ourselves.

New Year

Life and all the days we are spun
Lie secure in the hand
Of our Maker
Oh, yes bar none!

Harried lives, too full to be won
Are not designed by this
Rhythm Shaker
So, slow down some!

Gracefully in step with the Host
Who delights being the
Mercy Chaser
Give Him a toast!

Resolution to dance 'til done
Calls for strong signals from
The Peace Pacer
Pray ye often!

A whole New Year! Ours to welcome
Full of shalom from the
World's Dream Baser
Wow! How awesome!

Dependable Deliverer

Sure-footed, sure fired, sure thing, sure-enough
    Trusty, trustable with life's precious stuff
Here and there, yes, everywhere in the world
    Our deliverer is coming!
    Let your flag be unfurled!

Uncertain, unreliable, unsound
    Dubious, doubtful, dank and hell-bound
Automated sin-handling won't do
    The deceiver is prowling!
    Will God's mail get through?

Rejoice, re-affirm, reconnect, re-stamp
    Exclaim, exult, that your soul's on the map!
Cross-wise method can reach every heart
    Dependable deliverer
    Guaranteed from the start!

Voting Citizen

Born in Grant County in the dairy state
    Blessed a citizen of this grand union
Reborn in waters of the Lincoln state
    Made child of a heavenly reunion

One foot on earth the other in heaven
    My double burgher to taste and embrace
One tainted with poison from start to end
    The other pure oil—God's kingdom of grace

Oh, such rights and responsibilities!
    To vote for God's light while tears block my view
My mind drawn to short-lived, harsh realities
    While heart longs for love's voice and all things new

Still I press on to make heaven my own
    Setting my sights on that afterworld's call
That Lord of both spheres makes me His own
    I give my best now to welcome home all

New Day Coming

    New day coming
So what will we see beyond our purview?
      Warriors cease fire
      Hungry are fed
Smiles on the faces of loved ones long dead!

    Bells are ringing
What will tyros' ears hear in this new age?
      Belly laughter
      Songs of great joy
Fun words of thanksgiving gladly employed!

    Meals will be served
How will life taste when this new day occurs?
      Crisp and salty
      Toothsome dessert
Fresh fruit of Spirit raised out of sin's dirt!

    Incense rising
What will we sniff as old gifts are made new?
      Clean, rain fresh breeze
      Scent of baked bread
Aroma of world washed and mercy lead!

    God's human touch
Born and still comes bringing new life so that
      Neighbors embrace
      Enmity melts
Gone dreadful fear being lost we have felt!

    Soulful matter
What will we sense when the Lord's Day appears?
      Life is restored!
      Friendships sealed!
Hearts will all beat for God's love now revealed!

Robed and Ready

    All you behind
Locked doors stuck like glue
    Weight of the world
Pressing down hard on you
    Listen, you'll hear
Living Word tried and true
    Beginning and
End of things old and new

    Knock on your door?
'Tis One for all races!
    Voice of God's love
Filled with glory divine
    White flowing robes
And familiar faces
    Cast in the light
Of perpetual shine

    Come, you who've been
Through the great, dark ordeal
    Death of body
Yet, alive in the Lord
    See, now your home
Is with God who is real
    Wiping away
Tears of all who have mourned

    Heaven He'll bring
First earth must go its way
    Bright Son of God
Will stoop and give you peace
    Seated on throne
Your Savior comes to stay
    That you may be
Robed and ready to feast!

After the Fall

My eyes are wide open
    But I'm simply unaware
So I crash through again
    And the pain's so hard to bear!

How strange this lifeless place
    Where I have fallen heart-first
Searching for just a taste
    Am I now to die of thirst?

What is that sound I hear
    Coming from outside the door?
It is He shedding tears
    For me to be free and more!

Love like a master key
    Enters in with excitement
Rise, little one and see
    After the fall—atonement!

Holy Fusion

Oh, dreadful thought of that grim day
    Sudden release of energy
Sending shock waves every which way
    Fireball far as you can see

When it goes up who will be spared?
    Such explosive power—God's wrath!
The fallout of sin on skin bare
    Nowhere safe from its deadly path

Nowhere but the heart of the spark
    Where pure life elements unite
And holy fusion blows out the dark
    Love's inertia winning the fight

Early Easter, Late Day Snow

A child protests to her mother at the door,
"Bet God doesn't have to wear socks any more!"
"No," Mom says, "even **His** boots were left behind.
But we all need covers—both your feet and mine.
It's late winter outside. There's cold, wind and snow.
God wants us safe and warm, snug from head to toe!
One day we'll play barefoot in the park.
Full sun will come, and it won't be near dark."

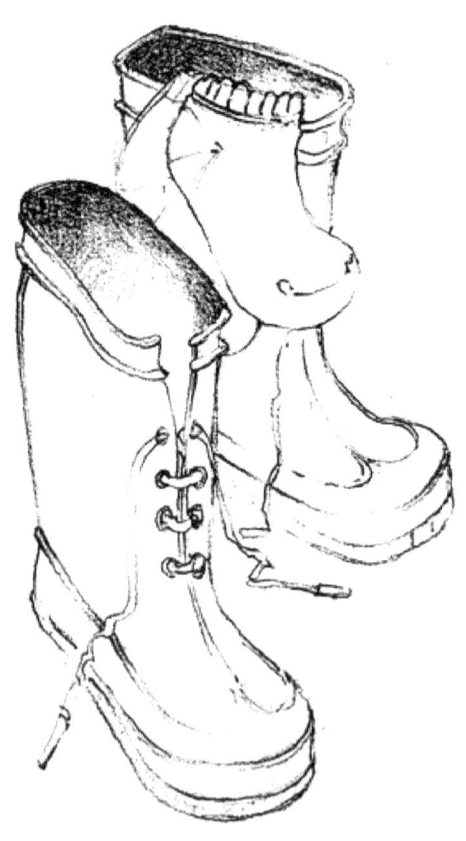

A Better Future

Past, present—a better future
    At least, I'm led to think it so
Lord, today bless all our bloopers
    And grant us what we need to show
Your heaven is much closer now
    A foretaste of the life You vow

Tidings of Hope

Behold, a new day dawning!
Can you see it?
In the glory of the cross!
Little children,
Open up your eyes and ears!
Let not fears of
Discord, hunger, sickness, death
Freeze you silent!

Hear God's glad tidings of hope!
Focus not on
Your problems alone but look!
Deliverance!
Self, belonging and purpose
All set in eternity
Life is more sure
Than the rising of the sun!

Oh, let eternity reign
In hearts and minds
That souls may soar like eagles!
As the day of the Lord draws near!

Be Now My Way

Sign says "Exit Only" and I enter
    Mind says, "ABSOLUTLY NO ENTRY!" yet
    nothing hinders
Heart skips a beat when the grave is open
    Soul says, "No!" but my ears are broken
Lord, guide me who strays.

Word speaks of One who never has to sleep
    Face of man meant to comfort those who weep
Mind goes blind while heart skips another beat
    Lord, come near I pray.

Cross sighs, "Dead End" yet faith says "Enter in"
    Self dies as voice cries, "You're sure to win!"
Heart skips a beat with death's defeat
    Soul says, "Yes!" to God's elite
Lord, be now my way!

Joy Awaits

Hiking a trail along the North Shore
Thoughts of what we will see at the end begin

Will we catch the best light of the day
Or will dark clouds hide our world with doom and gloom?

We trust the guide, strive, persevere and
Seek panoramic perspective's new view

Why? 'Cause this day as in the last day
Is a blessed day full of God's grace—Aced!

Joy awaits all those who walk by faith
Who face the unknown and in life distressed, rest

Shadow on the Sun Porch

There's a shadow on the sun porch
    That now looms bigger than life
Chilling our talk as shallow and forced
    We're stymied by fear of its sight

What must we make of this shadow?
    Its shade has us all up in arms
Cold, fall wind blows through the window
    The change in you sets off alarms

You are dying, Dad. Are you scared?
    Don't you wonder how this can be?
That a shadow moves here to there
    And we face the cold space between

But one has embraced this shadow
    Returned and declared it a friend!
And from dark shades of winter known
    Comes the warm spring of life God sends

    . . . See you in the garden, Dad.

When Shadows Fall

Oh risen Son
Key of the day!
Reveal the face of God
In your bright rays
Lest your people
Now be locked out
Light up the path for life
Save us from doubt
You, Day-Glow, who
Shines through the door
Of Heaven and Hades
Mercy in store
Be our watchword
For Kingdom's call
That we not be afraid
When shadows fall

Oh, Lasting City!

Oh, Lasting City, we seek You to come!
Amidst earthly shadows, Thy will be done!
While you, nitty-gritty, so void of faith
Home to nomadic clans' refuge and strength
Your grids for protection, movement at length
Now hell-bent on death and devil's sharp scathe!

Spiritual center of wind and water
Heart of true nature and all that matters
Creation cries for your way be made known
We long for this sacred geography!
Saint and citizens of eternity
Heaven full rural to urban atoned

Ah, Borough of Good, end of the cycle
Squared, covered by the strong arm of Michael
Inverted metropolis he slaughters!
But ours like Mother Divine Protectress
Forever giving that we may be blessed
Safe haven from wrath's fire and floodwaters!

Fall Faith

Three leaves on a stem
    Fall days once again
    River of grace
    Circle of life
    Fall on my lap

Breeze quickens the heart
    Sun warms the spirit
    Voice from within
    Joy stirs again
    Fall fills the gap

Diff'rent each season
    Four born from the One
    Each bearing gifts
    All for taking
    Fall's on the map

Dry grass needs water
    Cold comes, fall totters
    Can dead leaves live again?
    River of grace
    Circle of life
    Fall faith on tap

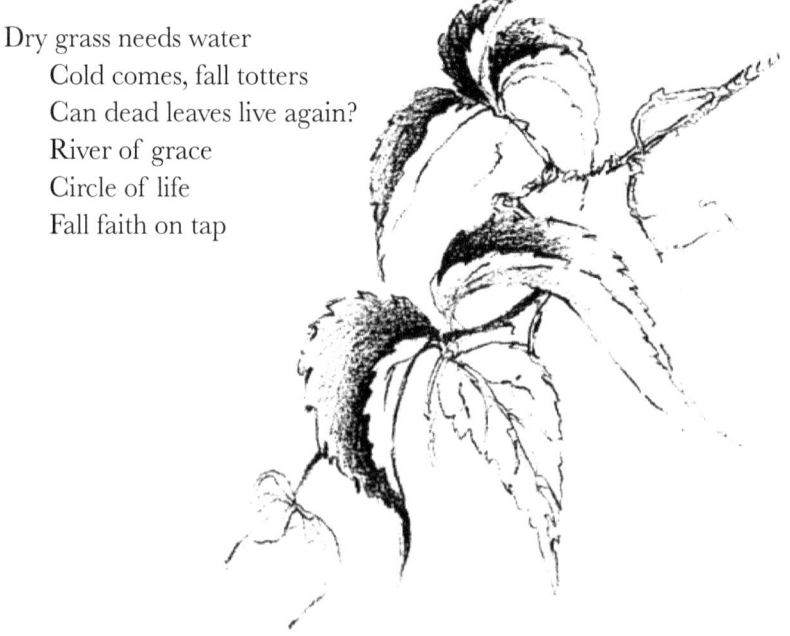

Wait and Trust

O
The
Agony
Young Eyes
On a tall, green tree
Waiting, waiting . . .
Seems like an eternity
For Christmas Day to come
It's that way at age ten
Yet, does the waiting ever end?
O Tree of both life and death
Ever rising to the heights of heaven
In springs of living water your roots rest
A leafy cross of hope and glory
That tells us all the world's love story
Waiting, waiting, waiting for Your peace
Star of all seasons shine upon us
That we may do what every child of light does
Love God and others as we wait and trust
'Til death—that latest time when Christ delivers us
Come,
Lord
Jesus!

A Closer Walk with Thee

Are there tennis courts in heaven?
Do you cook breakfast in the park?
Oh, I suppose it won't really matter
There will be plenty to do together

Together . . .
I do thank you
For the many times we shared together
The card games
Talks at the table
Pop at the bar
How about that time
We took a walk?

What ever possessed you
To wake me from my sleep?
One out of five
Four in the morning
You whispered,
"J.R., come with me."

In the near forty-four years I knew you
I don't know if there was
A more precious moment
Than that morning you called me
To take a walk in the dark
It was you wasn't it?
Tell me you had hold of
Every one of your faculties

But then I suppose
It really doesn't matter
For from before I was born
To your last November breath
God used you to reach me
And I realize now
You were the best dad you could be

So, I thank you, Lord, for the gift of my father
And I thank you for that walk in the dark
But I thank you most
For what we're still not sure of
Because I know now
That walk in the dark was certainly
Oh, yes, is and will be most certainly
A closer walk with thee!

Reflection/Discussion Questions

1. What resolutions have you made for this current year?

2. Who determines how well you are doing?

3. What signs do you look for that tells you how your future looks?

4. What visions and dreams inform your sense of what your future will be like?

5. How do you find the courage and confidence to face the unknown?

6. How have you dealt (or will you deal) with the death of loved ones?

7. What feelings surface when you think of your own death?

8. What gives you hope?

9. What helps you determine what is possible in your future?

10. Where do you think you're going after you die?

11. To whom do you entrust your future?

12. With whom would you like a "closer walk"?

Notes on Poems

Pilot Me
Sin is separation and alienation from our true identity that cuts off the lifeline of our souls and threatens to stop us short of reaching our destiny. Jesus is seen as The Pilot or Shepherd of souls who leads those willing unto lovely green pastures that nurture eternal life and develop grace-based identity.

Shame in the Weather
In shame-based existence, one fears exposure and has a difficult time reading the signs of emotional turbulence. The Son of God offers himself as a lightning rod grounding our toxic shame and turning our fears into healthy reverence and genuine humility.

Shifting Shadow
Pride can tempt us to deny God's grace rendering us an easy target for the devil's dart.

Legion at the Crossroads
Christ will cross our path often and most dramatically in our darkest hour. We listen for his still, quiet voice amidst fears that scream at us. One word of truth from the Son of God has the power to send every fear to flight and transform us from troubled captives among fearful tombs to freedom dancers announcing good news.

Winter's Thaw
A childhood memory of cutting a finger on a piece of glass becomes the poetic spark to help articulate a thaw in emotional numbness.

Monstrous Love
Some silly mark on the woodwork in the hallway outside a bedroom door took on a scary, evil life of its own for a small boy. Little did he

know that same fear would surface again in adulthood and require the overwhelming, supernatural power of God's love to overcome.

Black Hole

Recovery from any kind of addiction includes facing the fear of hitting bottom again.

Gospel Light

Darkness tends to threaten our choices, scare and immobilize. Light revealed through the Father, Son and Holy Spirit restores our confidence, reduces our fears and assures us eternal mobility.

Mutinous Emotion

Mutiny of emotions occurs when we loose confidence in the Captain of our souls.

Biffy by the Handle

This poem captures an epiphany experienced at the moment a grown man took hold of the handle on a portable outdoor toilet at Lake Harriet in Minneapolis. Having struggled for months with depression, he suddenly came in contact with a scared child within him longing for signs of divine love and approval.

Habits

Take heart. Cutting "new tapes" and developing new habits is tough work in recovery that takes a long time and calls for lots of patience—others' and especially our own.

Take Heart

Understanding what ails us is over-rated. The mind is limited in what it can think. The body is limited in how it can act. Only our soul can envision shalom and the health and wholeness that is available to us through sanctified imagination.

Notes on Poems

Mercy Seat

A place of atonement, where one can experience an "at-one-ment" with God is essential in every home.

Pan for Gold

To fully explore the river of life guarantees encountering rough waters. Spiritual riches lie beneath and beyond the most threatening waves.

Less Being More

Being overweight offers a valuable life lesson.

Mother Divine

Oh, the comfort of embracing the mother image of God!

Mother's Apron Strings

Maturity calls for the ability to stay meaningfully connected to our family of origin yet sufficiently detached. We never loose need of a healthy mothering source no matter what stage of life we are in.

Birthday Party

Birthdays were not celebrated much in this man's family of origin. All the more reason why his father taking time, money and effort to grant him a birthday party when he turned seven is something he will treasure forever.

Wave of Contractions

Memory and imagination are intimately related. The fact that this man's parents suffered a stillborn just prior to his birth but never talked much about it leaves much unsettled.

In Your Real Presence

Spiritual intuition is not limited to feelings that are fickle and quick to fade. A more constant sense of the divine is stirred by the beauty and warmth of God revealed to us through multiple means of grace everyday.

Cross Examination

The cross serves as a realistic frame of reference for our human condition; is a powerful sign of God's love and self-sacrifice, a precious key that opens to us a broader view of God's glory and a bottom line that reveals the staggering cost for God's gift of abundant life.

Listen to Him!

The Kingdom of God with a promise for peace breaks into our lives not by force but willing ears open to the word spoken by the Son of God.

Dark Side of Moon

We are not the light of God but we are privileged to bask in the light of God's grace and reflect God's love for others.

Name Change

Divine encounter stirs up new nameable life, purpose and identity.

Dawn of My Real Mother

Only the steadfast love and protection of our mothering God will not faint or grow weary.

Built on The Rock

On our own we are unable to overcome approval addiction. Only by a spiritual power greater than we are can we build our lives on solid ground and choose a different path to walk than the slippery slopes of co-dependency.

Saved from Grandiosity

Children asked to bear adult-size hardship and responsibility are set up for failure and often left with toxic shame.

Notes on Poems

Rabbouni!

The risen Christ would do little to empower our lives were it not for his personal touch through the quickened lives of those around us.

Save Me!

The ego we try to construct by identification with God substitutes will sink like a stone in the river of life.

Tug – of – War

Internal conflict will often arise. What a relief to discover Jesus' winning influence!

Found

God always initiates. To "find God" is to respond to life with faith, hope and love.

Curl Unfurled

As goes the slogan used in many recovery groups: "Let go and let God."

Pup in Arms

The child in every one of us has been traumatized to one extent or another. The inspiration God sends to minister to that child comes in every imaginable shape, size and color.

Holy Volition

God gives us choices. Anything, certainly to include television, which numbs our senses and weakens our will to choose meaningful, heart-to-heart dialogue with God and others is a drug potentially dangerous to our health and to the health of those around us.

Cataclysmic Party Prep

Thorough house cleaning can appear quite violent upending furniture, taking down curtains, pulling up carpet, trashing things that have been around for years. As in homes so in hearts, from time to time a thorough cleaning is needed in spite of it being more invasive than most people would like.

Christmas Dinner

While in Western eyes the elephant is the picture of overweight clumsiness, the Eastern image is quite different. Elephants were ridden by kings and most notably by the Lord of the Heavens. So, while an elephant at the dinner table may symbolize a serious threat in the family of an alcoholic, Christmas brings the glad announcement that unto us comes the King of Kings, Lord of the Heavens who is able to tame and harness even the biggest threats to our peace and well being.

Wedding Gift

Imagine how many divorces could be avoided if every husband and wife would first learn to tend to the child in themselves before bringing other children into the world.

Marital Dawn of Men and Women

Marriage is a life-long commitment to collaboration, wife and husband validating and strengthening each other that each may reach their full God-given potential and together realize that greatest of all gifts—love.

Embryo Maker

God is the author of all beginnings, the wind that breathes life into the undeveloped state of every good thing. In Christ, what God begins is brought to completion.

His Holy Break

Picture a young, teenage boy seeking relief from manic-depression in a bout with drunkenness. Add in the death of his father at age four, a bedridden mother by age thirteen and the economic disaster of his family's orchard in the Great Depression. Now watch this boy driving an old, beat up truck loaded with fresh peaches sail down a steep hill only to find he has no brakes.

Notes on Poems

Surefooted Grace

A dream spawned this horrible image of shame-based vertigo. Any attempt to control another's co-dependency is as futile as a little child trying to hold his parents upright as their ladder falls backwards.

Case of Empty Promises

Oh, the pain that vows can deliver! A grace-based promise is the only one we dare count on.

Red Pop

Long after much of a bad childhood memory fades, the red face of anger and shame remain deeply emblazed on one's mind and heart; so also that flu-like feeling in the gut.

Strong in the Song

Song is the symbol of that strong link between us and the breath of life. It is the creature's voice responding to the Creator, the object of our joy and worship. It is the language of prayer grounded in ultimate truth.

Wholly Begotten!

The biblical story of the prodigal son encourages both those at home and "on the road." By grace we are empowered to love like the Father and to be loved like the son.

Diamonds

While the monetary value of diamonds can vary considerably, the symbolism of a diamond's strength and immutability is constant, universal and priceless. Diamonds also point to the peak of spiritual development.

Joy-o-meter

To gain an accurate reading of one's own feelings is a difficult task for anyone who suffers from co-dependency. That God loved us enough to die on the cross does, however, provide the necessary baseline for truth and recovery.

Just Grateful

Gratitude points to and embraces grace and it is God's grace that saves us.

Beckoning

Goose Lake is located in the Elm Creek Preserve, 4,500 acres of lovely rolling prairie on the north end of Hennepin County in Minnesota.

Catch the Wonder

This was a song written and performed at Holden Village in the state of Washington.

God's Smile

We discover our full potential in the light of God's unconditional, loving smile turned toward us.

In My Mist

Mystery magnifies God's glory and explains why human kind, made in God's image, can never be fully understood or appreciated.

Clouds over my Head

Our notion of divinity and the nature of things is not a world of either/or but both inner and outer, mind and matter, fact and imagination.

Gooey Ducks

To an Iowa boy new to the Washington coast for college, digging up long-neck clams and roasting them by the ocean was a bold venture into a whole new wonderful and exciting world.

Notes on Poems

Hopper in the Grass

With God nothing is impossible!

Pearl of Great Price

Life's richest treasures are born out of pain and suffering.

True Friendship

Etymologically, *friend* means 'loving' and God is love.

Trinity

The essence of God's divinity is not fully revealed in this threefold unity, but it helps reconcile our worship of Christ with monotheism and better enables us to personally identify with the One who creates, redeems and sanctifies.

Born Again

Ego is born out of necessity for life in this world. Selfhood is reborn for eternal life as ego gives way to the soul quickened by the love of God.

Seattle

Spotting a grandchild captivated by bulldozers and cranes, the Space Needle and Puget Sound proved contagious, fueling the flame for life-long learning.

Mount Tallac

Inspired by a mountain climb above Lake Tahoe, thoughts of Christ sweating blood for the tiny space we fill proved the mountain high.

Choir of Waterfalls

During a summer visit to Norway we came through a long tunnel out into the Fjærland Valley surrounded by a glacier rim. A beautiful sound of waterfalls stirred the love and friendship my wife Denise and I have shared for years with Norwegian friends, Marianne and

Notes on Poems

Thor Henrik With, and reminded us of the peace that awaits us in heaven.

Midnight Sun

It was June, just before 12 o'clock at night. Together with Norwegian friends, Gerde Helena Bolme and her husband Kjell, Denise and I climbed atop a hill in their town of Bodø, in northern Norway. There we giggled and danced, hugged and took pictures as we basked in the light of the midnight sun.

Duck Pond Dawn

This poem is dedicated to my father-in-law, Greg Beemer, who drew my attention to a glorious sunrise over a pond outside our window the morning after an early summer thunderstorm.

Bird Tale

Creativity calls for child-like foolishness, betting on the outside chance of capturing something wonderful.

Minnesota Lake Place and *Dance at the Lake*

These and other poems were written at our friend, Rita Larson's lake place on Sugar Bay of Crooked Lake, northwest of Garrison, Minnesota. Thank God for generous friends and for the beauty of creation!

Lovely Lambent Server

In the flickering candlelight of a rustic restaurant a lovely server brought hot coffee to a table by a window. Outside, stars shone brightly. Imagination was ignited and the Christ child was born anew!

Sacred Walking

A labyrinth is a circular maze within which one may move slowly and meditate. Liken to modern satellite navigation, walking a labyrinth connects with a source that enlightens and empowers soul travel.

Notes on Poems

This and More

By no means limited by what we know, God is not confined to mystery either. The fullness of reality is realized by the limitlessness of God made known to us through the profound synergism of both faith and facts.

State to State

Inspiration comes readily on the beautiful north shores of Lake Superior. Such can awaken hearts to be stirred in daily life, prompting us to act beneficently out of gratitude deep in our soul.

Better Beauty

My, how life lived by a theology of glory fades fast in the light of God's love on the cross!

Tunneling

The ability to envision stark beauty through the end of a long dark tunnel was awakened by road travel in Norway.

Clear as Broad Daylight

A mix of metaphors and blend of senses may seem cacophonous in the din of literalism but can prove melodious and soothing for the liberated soul.

Frost

Elm Creek Preserve provides a place to walk through stages of grief necessary to embrace a change of seasons.

Wonderful Names Wondrous Lord!

This string of haiku poems are like prayer beads connecting us to the vastness of God with brevity and concreteness.

Community

In the hunt for true community trust is essential.

Welcome to the Neighborhood!

Made in the image of the triune God, we are communal by nature.

Raising Up Fun

For the adult child of a chronically traumatized family, fun can seem like a forbidden luxury. Thankfully, support groups committed to helping people discover the fun-loving child within are available today in many communities.

Leader Led

How to lead effectively occupies the secular mind. The art of leadership that makes a lasting and profound difference calls for attention and care of the soul.

Hallowed Mission Statement

The popularity of a mission statement can be misleading. The word structure becomes a "no-god" if it turns out to be a shinning statement on a wall rather than a personal and moving mandate on the heart.

God's Gift of Community

The vision we cast of God's vast faith community reveals a future already at hand entrusted to humble servants willing and confident to trust in the power of their tweaks.

Living in the Tension

There appears to be no "tension-free" zone this side of God's Kingdom.

Miracle on the Hill and *Thrills and Chills*

Daughter Toby was born at Group Health Hospital on Capital Hill in Seattle. Daughter Brooke was born at Hennepin County Medical Center in Minneapolis. Each has her own gifts and challenges. Both have given their parents opportunity to experience a full range of

Notes on Poems

parental joys and sorrows. What comfort to know children and parents alike are forever secure in the arms of God's grace!

Lost No More

Moved by her gift of a beautiful cross-stitch portrait of our loving Shepherd, this little poem was written for and dedicated to my friend and our congregation's beloved parish nurse, Diane Wenninger.

Claim It and Act!

Consider the man who held the winning lottery ticket, good for millions of dollars after taxes, hidden in his wallet for days. Such a story gave rise to this poetic prod.

Ticket to Significance

By my brother Gary's gracious invitation, I learned to play guitar and sing rock n roll in the early 60s. After several years in my brother's group, the El Dorados, I moved on to help form The Jesters. In the late 60s, at the height of my rock music career, the Jesters evolved into the Butterscotch Grove and our vehicle for road trips became a psychedelic bus.

My Caribou

I have the local Caribou Coffee © shop to thank for helping stimulate much of my creative writing!

Headed for Bodø

By the time our soul train passed through the last stunning snow and rainbow decorated mountain range and valley and we rolled over the idyllic and much acclaimed Norwegian Arctic Circle, a joyful, new and diverse community was born.

Visit to Røsvik

What a privilege to have had this precious story told to us by members of Gerde Helena Bolme's family while visiting her grandparent's home near the shores of northern Norway. May God bless all memories of loved ones lost at sea.

Human Race

To what end do we compete and how do we measure a win? The prize for which God calls us comes by way of a joint effort in which everyone is included and even the last are first.

Campfire

I have the people of Wapogasset Lutheran Bible Camp near Amery, Wisconsin to thank for introducing me to the wonderful and spirited world of campfire communities.

Hospital Calls

This poem is dedicated to all those who work in one capacity or another in hospital communities, embodying the love and healing presence of the Great Physician.

Christ's Heart

In the catalogue of life there is good, better and best and the greatest of these is what we gladly give others as unto the Lord.

God So Loves Them!

These words were written and sung for Siri Knutson and Dan Drontle at their wedding ceremony on September 30, 2006 in the chapel at Mount Carmel Bible Camp near Alexandria, Minnesota.

Crows on a Crossbeam

Widely believed a sign of imminent destruction, the message of the crow is transformed from doom and gloom to hope and joy by the power of the Cross.

Pentecostal Delight

African and Latino Pentecostals have enriched the lives of many long-standing Lutherans of Northern European descent in the mission partnership we share at Cross of Glory Lutheran Church in Brooklyn Center, Minnesota. This poem is dedicated to my dear Liberian friend, Bishop Alfred Reeves, and the vision we share of a world united in Christ.

A Good Boat

A boat is a symbolic cradle for the soul. Like a boat the Church is seen as the means of transition from earth to one's home in heaven.

A Fresh New Start

The Spirit of God stirs up the ability to imagine, opens the mind's eye to see what God makes possible and warms the heart to seek fellowship with God and others.

New Year

To welcome God as the "First Foot" into every New Year reveals to us countless reasons for which to celebrate and opens the door for the blessings in store.

Dependable Deliverer

Mail handlers have impressed us for years. What they do to get love lines and care packages through to us is amazing! Still more amazing is the way God gets through to every longing heart no matter what, when or where, choosing to reach us in flesh and spirit rather than rely on mere words printed on a page.

Voting Citizen

To be citizens of both heaven and earth lends to frequent conflicts of interest and everyday bouts with ambiguity. But to be homeless and without voice; this must certainly feel like hell!

New Day Coming

Joyful images burst like buttered popcorn when we dare believe in the promises of God in spite of our unbelief.

Notes on Poems

Robed and Ready

Though able to penetrate dead bolted doors, our Lord more often chooses to wait on us to open our hearts and entrust ourselves to his saving presence. Welcoming him with a believing heart, like the mysterious nature of Holy Communion, calls for opening ourselves to be transformed, no longer mere flesh subject to sin but a bride adorned, heavenly saints robed and ready to feast at his heavenly banquet table.

After the Fall

The story of a curious cat falling through my mother-in-law, Donna Beemer's roof in San Jose', California led to this poetic portrayal of sin and redemption.

Holy Fusion

The explosive power of God's wrath always serves to create new life!

Early Easter, Late Day Snow

The barrier that separates life on earth from life in heaven melts like snow when we embrace the Son of God like a warm, loving mother's wise protection and faithful promise.

A Better Future

Sanctification is a process that builds on the best today for a better tomorrow. Each day God provides us a foretaste of the life yet to come.

Tidings of Hope

The heart of all hope is based on the disputed fact that Christ rose from the dead. Our belief in the resurrection, in spite of unbelief, blows wind into the sails of our soul!

Notes on Poems

Be Now My Way

Signs can be confusing. Often we are tempted to discard them; to come and go as we please. This is why to be a devoted follower of Jesus Christ is often not easy. Thankfully, Christ assures he will be with us always, making God's way possible for us all.

Joy Awaits

Hiking in areas where weather changes by the minute and can make or break the journey requires an element of faith not unlike that which motivates and empowers us to seek day by day the beauty of the Lord.

Shadow on the Sun Porch and *When Shadows Fall*

Shadows are often associated with scary spirits from the underworld. In Christ, the most fearsome shadow can be owned, our fears cast out, and even death befriended.

Oh, Lasting City!

In the City of God, not too long from now, all will be safe, sane and forever satisfied.

Fall Faith

This playful little poem does not capture the significance of the incident that led to it being written. Three brown leaves on a stem fell into a man's lap one warm fall afternoon as he sat on a bench on the banks of the Mississippi River. This he believed was a sign sent from above delivering unto him this blessed assurance: God who takes note of every leaf that falls will surely care and comfort him on the day he cascades to the ground. And as he watched the river flow from one season to the next, a wave of great joy came over him.

Wait and Trust

Each season teaches us valuable lessons for soulful living. The season of Advent is no exception. To gain a greater appreciation for the spiritual benefits of waiting on the Lord holds out promise for a host of heavenly dividends.

A Closer Walk with Thee

We need not suffer want of a better parent when in faith every mom, dad, and guardian, regardless of their ability to lovingly raise a child points us to the perfect parent we are blessed to have for eternity.

Index of Titles

A

A Better Future 139
A Closer Walk with Thee 148
A Fresh New Start 126
A Good Boat 124
After the Fall 136

B

Be Now My Way 141
Beckoning 65
Better Beauty 90
Biffy by the Handle 15
Bird Tale 83
Birthday Party 24
Black Hole 12
Born Again 76
Built on The Rock 32

C

Campfire 118
Case of Empty Promises 52
Cataclysmic Party Prep 42
Catch the Wonder 66
Choir of Waterfalls 80
Christmas Dinner 43
Christ's Heart 120
Claim It and Act! 109
Clear as Broad Daylight 92
Clouds over my Head 70
Community 98
Cross Examination 27
Crows on a Crossbeam 122
Curl Unfurled 39

D

Dance at the Lake 84
Dark Side of Moon 28
Dawn of My Real Mother 30
Dependable Deliverer 132

Diamonds 59
Duck Pond Dawn 82

E

Early Easter, Late Day Snow 138
Embryo Maker 47

F

Fall Faith 146
Found 38
Frost 93

G

God So Loves Them! 121
God's Smile 68
God's Gift of Community 103
Gooey Ducks 71
Gospel Light 13

H

Habits 17
Hallowed Mission Statement 102
Headed for Bodø 113
His Holy Break 49
Holy Fusion 137
Holy Volition 41
Hopper in the Grass 72
Hospital Calls 119
Human Race 117

I

In My Mist 69
In Your Real Presence 27

J

Joy Awaits 142
Joy-o-meter 60
Just Grateful 61

Index of Titles and Subjects

L

Leader Led 101
Legion at the Crossroads 6
Less Being More 21
Listen to Him! 28
Living in the Tension 104
Lost No More 108
Lovely Lambent Server 85

M

Marital Dawn of Men and
 Women 46
Mercy Seat 19
Midnight Sun 81
Minnesota Lake Place 84
Miracle on a Hill 105
Monstrous Love 10
Mother Divine 22
Mother's Apron Strings 23
Mount Tallac 79
Mutinous Emotion 14
My Caribou 112

N

Name Change 29
New Day Coming 134
New Year 131

O

Oh, Lasting City! 145

P

Pan for Gold 20
Pearl of Great Price 73
Pentecostal Delight 123
Pilot Me 3
Pup in Arms 40

R

Rabbouni! 34
Raising Up Fun 100

Red Pop 54
Robed and Ready 135

S

Sacred Walking 87
Save Me! 35
Saved from Grandiosity 33
Seattle 77
Shadow on the Sun Porch 143
Shame in the Weather 4
Shifting Shadow 5
State to State 89
Strong in the Song 55
Surefooted Grace 51

T

Take Heart 18
This and More 88
Thrills and Chills 106
Ticket to Significance 110
Tidings of Hope 140
Trinity 75
True Friendship 74
Tug – of – War 36
Tunneling 91

V

Visit to Røsvik 115
Voting Citizen 133

W

Wait and Trust 147
Wave of Contractions 26
Wedding Gift 45
Welcome to the Neighborhood! 99
When Shadows Fall 144
Wholly Begotten! 57
Winter's Thaw 8
Wonderful Names,
 Wondrous Lord! 94

www.ingramcontent.com/pod-product-compliance
Lightning Source LLC
Chambersburg PA
CBHW051931160426
43198CB00012B/2110